BREAKING THE GRIP OF ANXIETY

Reclaim Your Mind And Discover Peace

Tom Flores

LIFE PUBLISHING HOUSE

All Scripture quotations are taken from the *New King James Version*®. Copyright © 1982 by Thomas Nelson. Used by permission. All rights reserved.

Unless otherwise indicated, all emphasis in Scripture quotations is the author's.

Publisher: LIFE PUBLISHING HOUSE

This book is intended for inspirational and educational purposes only. The author and publisher do not dispense medical, psychological, or professional counseling advice. Readers are encouraged to seek professional help when needed. The views expressed are those of the author.

ISBN: 979-8-9942828-1-6
Printed in the United States of America

Contents

Introduction

Anxiety is one of the greatest silent battles people face today. Many struggle quietly behind closed doors while trying to appear strong on the outside. Some battle racing thoughts that never seem to stop. Others live with constant fear, pressure, stress, panic, sleepless nights, or emotional exhaustion. Anxiety can affect every part of a person's life, including the mind, body, relationships, decisions, emotions, and even faith. It can make someone feel trapped inside their own thoughts and overwhelmed by things they cannot seem to control.

I know this struggle personally. There was a time in my life when anxiety became very real to me. Outwardly, life may have looked normal, but inwardly I was carrying fear, pressure, stress, and constant overthinking. My mind felt exhausted at times, and peace seemed difficult to hold onto. Anxiety has a way of making a person feel isolated, drained, and stuck in cycles that seem impossible to break. It can convince you that things will never change and that fear will always control your life.

But through my own journey, I discovered something important: anxiety does not have to win. As I searched for answers, God began showing me practical and spiritual tools that helped me overcome anxiety and renew my mind. I learned that healing was not about pretending everything was fine or ignoring what I felt. It was about confronting unhealthy thought patterns, understanding how fear operates, applying God's Word daily, learning to trust Him in deeper ways, and allowing His truth to reshape my thinking. Through prayer, Scripture, practical wisdom, and God's presence, I slowly began experiencing freedom and peace again.

This book was born out of that journey. *Breaking The Grip Of Anxiety* is not written from a place of theory alone. It was written from experience, study, prayer, and a deep desire to help people who are fighting the same battles I once faced. My goal is to bring understanding, hope, healing, and practical direction to anyone that is dealing with anxiety. Anxiety is not always a sign of a lack of faith. Sometimes it develops through trauma, stress, fear, emotional wounds, exhaustion, or years of unhealthy thinking patterns. Even strong believers can wrestle with anxiety while still loving God deeply.

The title of this book comes from the powerful words found in **Philippians 4:6-7**: *"Be anxious for nothing, but in everything by prayer and supplication, with thanksgiving,* *let your requests be made known to God; and the peace of God, which surpasses all understanding, will guard your hearts and minds through Christ Jesus."* God never ignores the reality of anxiety, but He also never intended for anxiety to rule our lives. His Word offers peace, wisdom, healing, and hope for those who feel overwhelmed.

In these pages, we will explore what anxiety is, how it affects the mind and body, where it comes from, and how it slowly gains influence over a person's life. More importantly, we will look at how God's truth can renew the mind, break destructive cycles, and restore peace where fear once ruled.

If you are tired of living controlled by fear, worry, panic, or emotional exhaustion, I want you to know there is hope. Freedom is possible. Peace is possible. Healing is possible. No matter how long anxiety has held onto your life, it does not have to define your future.

My prayer is that as you read this book, you will not only gain understanding, but also discover the peace that God promises to those who trust Him. You do not have to remain trapped in anxiety. Through God's truth and practical application, your mind can be renewed, your heart can heal, and your life can change.

Chapter 1

When What I Learned Wasn't Enough

I never imagined that I would one day write a book on anxiety. In the world I grew up in, I was taught that depression and anxiety were always attacks of the enemy and should be confronted only through spiritual means.

I was taught that a Christian should never need the help of a therapist, and medication was viewed as completely forbidden for believers. In my early years of ministry, I repeated what I had been taught. I believed that strong faith alone should be enough, that prayer alone should break every chain, and that if someone struggled with anxiety it was only because the enemy was working or their faith was not where it should be.

Then one morning everything changed for me. I woke up overwhelmed by a heaviness I had never experienced before. My thoughts were racing and fear gripped me before I could even get out of bed. I did everything I had been trained to do. I prayed. I read my Bible. Had hands laid on me. I quoted Scripture. I rebuked fear. I declared victory. But nothing seemed to work.

Day after day I felt myself sinking deeper into a place I could not climb out of. I had been fighting battle after battle with less and less strength until I reached a point where I could barely gather enough energy to read even one verse. My prayers felt hollow, and I was exhausted. Eventually I slipped into a depression I never believed someone like me could experience.

It was in that dark season, when prayer alone would not move the mountain I was facing, that my understanding began to shift. As I reached for help in ways I had never considered before, I started discovering truths that surprised me. I learned that many Christians, including pastors I knew and respected, quietly see therapists. I learned that faithful believers seek counseling because they genuinely want healing but do not know how to begin. I learned that some even use medication in seasons when anxiety becomes so overwhelming they can barely function. None of these people had a lack faith. They were simply human.

This realization began unraveling something in me. I started to see how often we can place unnecessary shame on someone who is hurting above the neckline. In the church we freely encourage believers to seek medical help when their bodies are injured or sick. If someone has high blood pressure, diabetes, heart problems, or chronic pain, we have no hesitation recommending a doctor. We pray for them, yes, but we also believe God works through medical professionals. Yet when it comes to the mind, everything changes. If the battle is physical, we allow treatment. If the battle is mental or emotional, we often label it as purely spiritual. We tell people to pray harder, confess more Scripture, or push through in silence. We unintentionally create an environment where people who are suffering feel too ashamed to ask for the help they desperately need.

In the middle of my own breaking point, God gently reminded me of something simple but profound. The brain is an organ. It can become overwhelmed just like any other part of the body. It can be affected by trauma, grief, stress, chemical imbalance, and years of unaddressed pressure. Just as the heart can fail, the mind can falter. Just as the body needs support to heal, sometimes the mind does too. This understanding opened my eyes to the truth that the God who formed our spirit also formed our mind, and the same God who heals through miracles also heals through wisdom, counsel, and the hands of those He has equipped for this very purpose.

Sitting with a trusted therapist does not replace the presence of God. It invites God into places we have closed off for years. Medication does not replace prayer. But it can stabilize the mind so the soul can finally breathe, reflect, and heal. For me, this journey did not represent a lack of faith, but a fuller embracing of it. It allowed me to see the breadth of God's compassion and the many ways He chooses to bring healing.

This book is not written by someone who has never struggled. It is written by someone who has lived it, walked through it, and walked with countless others facing the same battles. It is written by someone who discovered that the God who heals does not limit His methods. He heals through prayer. He heals through Scripture. He heals through community. He heals through professionals He has gifted to help untangle the places where our minds have been wounded or overwhelmed.

If you have ever felt ashamed for feeling anxious, you are not alone. If you have ever felt spiritually defeated because you needed help, you are not alone. If you have ever believed that something must be wrong with you because prayer did not instantly make the anxiety disappear, you are not alone. I pray that this book will bring hope, and help you discover what I learned later than I wish I had. God is not disappointed in your struggle. He is present in it. And He offers healing in every way His wisdom provides.

Chapter 2

Where Anxiety Begins

For a long time anxiety was real to me. I loved God, and I trusted Him, yet there were moments when my emotions did not line up with what I believed. That created a tension inside of me that i couldn't explain. On the outside, I had faith. On the inside, I was wrestling with fear.

What made it even harder was what I had been taught over the years. I carried this idea that as a believer, I should not experience anxiety at all. That if my trust in God was strong enough, these feelings would not show up. So when they did, I did not talk about it. I pushed it down and I tried to handle it quietly.

It became a silent burden. Because it felt like something I was not supposed to admit.

Because of this, Christians often suffer quietly. I have personally witnessed many who have gone to prayer meetings, hoping for relief. Only to find themselves still struggling in the area of fear and anxiety. They attend spiritual warfare gatherings, believing that something spiritual must be wrong. They ask for hands to be laid on them, hoping that one moment of prayer will silence the storm inside. Some even begin to wonder if they have a demon simply because they cannot explain why they feel the way they do.

Now it is true that unhealed wounds are often the very places where spiritual battles are most intensely felt. The enemy is always strategically looking for areas of past pain, rejection, or trauma and attempts to use those openings to create influence, confusion, and ongoing distress. In those moments, the enemy works subtly—exposing, amplifying, and manipulating those wounds to keep a person bound in cycles of fear and anxiety. He is skilled at exploiting what still hurts. This is why healing matters so deeply.

While I do not believe a truly born-again believer can be demon-possessed. Scripture and pastoral experience both affirm that believers can experience spiritual oppression, particularly in areas where fear, hurt, or unresolved pain remain. A spirit of fear, discouragement, or heaviness often targets those vulnerable places.

At the same time, not every struggle should be immediately labeled a direct spiritual attack. Many of the battles people face may not be connected to a demonic presence at all, but to past trauma that has never been fully healed.

I want you to know that far more Christians experience

anxiety than most people realize. I have met believers who love God wholeheartedly and still wake up with fear gripping them. I have witnessed pastors who lead large congregations walk through seasons of overwhelming anxiety behind closed doors. They speak hope to thousands while fighting battles in the secret places of their own soul.

This creates a deep confusion for the believer. How can someone who is filled with the Holy Spirit still feel afraid. How can someone who trusts God still experience mental stress that do not make sense. How can someone cling to the promises of Scripture yet feel their body respond as if danger is still present.

Anxiety can be confusing because it does not always follow a clear pattern. It can rise when life is good, when faith is strong, and when everything appears calm on the surface. That confusion often leads believers to question themselves. They wonder if their faith is flawed or if something is wrong with them when the truth is far more complex.

Much of the anxiety people face today is not about today at all. It is connected to past struggles, wounds, trauma, and hurts that were buried instead of healed. These were moments the heart was never designed to handle alone. What was suppressed for survival often resurfaces later as anxiety, tension, and emotional weight.

When I was growing up, my life was not steady. It was

not calm, predictable, or safe. There were moments of fear that came without warning, moments of confusion that left me trying to make sense of a world that felt too big and too broken, and moments of loss that carved deeper wounds than I could ever explain. In my book *The God Who Heals My Wounds* I wrote about how early pain can shape us. I described the ache of feeling unprotected, the weight of carrying things no child should ever have to carry, and the way trauma settles quietly into the corners of your soul.

One of the wounds that marked my childhood in a profound way was this. I was molested at a young age. At the time, I didn't understand what had happened or why it left me feeling afraid and confused, but the impact of that moment lived inside me long before I had the courage or clarity to talk about it. That violation taught my mind and body to stay on edge. It whispered that safety could disappear without warning. It shaped the way I viewed myself and the world around me. Even though I buried it deeply, it began shaping my nervous system before I ever knew what anxiety was. That hidden wound became part of the foundation of my emotional world.

I was young when my father died, but I was old enough to feel the weight of it. Old enough to feel the ground shift under me. Old enough to sense that something essential was suddenly gone. The silence that followed his death filled the house in a way I still remember. I remember watching the world continue around me as if nothing had happened, while everything inside me felt as if it had stopped. You don't realize how much you rely on the presence of a father until that presence is gone. When that foundation cracks, you are forced to build your life on unstable ground.

The loss of my brothers came later and cut even deeper. One of my brothers was murdered, and the shock of that moment ripped through our family like a storm we are still recovering from. It happened on Thanksgiving Day, a day meant for gratitude and gathering, but instead it became the day everything inside our home broke apart. I remember watching my mother collapse under the weight of it. Her grief carried a pain I never forgot. In the years that followed, I watched her sink into a deep depression. It took everything from her. She couldn't function, couldn't work, and slowly we lost everything we had. Eventually we became homeless. As a young boy, watching my mother fall apart, created a wound inside me that I carried for years.

My other brother died of leukemia. His death was different, slow and suffocating in a way that stretched across months and years. Watching someone you love fade before your eyes leaves a different kind of scar. It breaks you gently but deeply. It exhausts the soul in places you don't talk about. Losing both of them in such different ways created a weight inside me that I didn't know how to carry.

Those childhood moments didn't simply hurt me. They formed me. They created the framework through which I learned to interpret life. When you grow up watching chaos, you learn to wait for it. When you grow up feeling unsafe, your body learns to stay on guard. When you grow up holding grief, loss, and secrets too heavy for a child to carry, you learn to expect more of it. Eventually you stop breathing freely and begin living like the next blow is already on its way.

At the time, I didn't know that my nervous system was being shaped by every moment of fear and confusion. My body was learning to stay alert even in calm moments. I lived as if danger was always one step away. That posture became automatic. What I believed was my personality was actually self protection. What I thought was simply the way I was created to be was really the result of a heart trying to survive what it lived through. Anxiety didn't begin later in life. It began in the shadows of childhood long before I understood what any of it meant.

Some wounds arrive quietly. Others tear something open inside you. And then there are the losses that change you forever. Losing my father and losing both of my brothers became losses that settled deep within me. They became part of the landscape of my heart whether I admitted it or not.

I didn't know what to do with all of that pain, so I did

the only thing I knew how to do. I got busy. I buried myself in life and ministry. I told myself that serving, working, and staying in constant motion meant I was doing the right thing. In reality, I was using busyness as an escape. I didn't deal with the pain. I didn't process the trauma. I kept moving because slowing down meant facing emotions I wasn't ready to confront.

Their deaths tore pieces out of me. They left empty spaces where memories should have lived. They were part of my history, part of my childhood, and part of the only sense of family structure I understood. When they were gone, something inside me fell silent. I didn't know how to process any of it, so I didn't. I carried it quietly, secretly, and heavily. It felt as if life kept taking pieces of me, and I had no way of getting them back.

People imagine that someone who experiences deep loss will fall apart, but I didn't. Not outwardly. I didn't break down the way many expected. I didn't collapse under the weight of it. I did what I had always done. I buried the pain and convinced myself that faithfulness and busyness were the same thing as healing. I hid hurt under responsibilities. I hid grief under activity. I hid trauma under a schedule that left no room for silence. I told myself that I was fine and that time had taken the sting away. I thought the past was behind me, but it lived inside me like something buried beneath the floorboards of my life.

But buried pain never disappears. It waits. It hides. It shapes the way you think and the way you react. It influences your fears, your beliefs, your relationships, and even the way you see yourself. I had lost so much, but instead of grieving I simply survived. But surviving is not the same thing as healing.

As I grew older, I convinced myself that I had outgrown the pain. I believed that the years had softened the wounds. I laughed, I worked, I built a life, I led others, and I encouraged people to face their own battles. All the while I kept mine hidden. But pain that is buried alive always finds its way back to the surface. My anxiety wasn't random. It was the voice of my past calling out for attention.

For years I didn't see the connection. I believed something was wrong with me. I believed I was weak. I believed my mind was broken. But my anxiety was the sign of a heart carrying losses I had never allowed myself to mourn.

Eventually there comes a moment when the weight of everything you have buried can no longer be held back. For me, it didn't happen in public. It didn't happen in the middle of a crisis. It happened in silence. I remember sitting alone on a quiet night when the pressure inside me felt unbearable. I felt overwhelmed, even though nothing around me was actually wrong. It was the most confusing kind of fear, because it didn't match the moment I was in. I had spent my entire life surviving, never learning how to heal. It was unprocessed grief that had waited years for me to finally acknowledge it.

Before you move further into this book, I want to speak directly to you. You are not weak. You are not broken. You are not losing your mind. What you feel is real. Your pain is valid. Anxiety may be strong, but it is not permanent. The grip of anxiety on your life can and will loosen. It happens one truth at a time, one breath at a time, one courageous step at a time.

As you continue reading, I pray you feel understood. I pray you find words for what you have carried in silence. I want you to know this with all your heart that freedom is closer than you think. I have walked this road, and I am still walking it. You are not alone. We are walking together toward a life where anxiety does not get the final word.

Chapter 3

Understanding Anxiety

Anxiety is a profound and complex human experience that reaches far beyond ordinary worry or nervousness. It is more than nervousness, more than worry, and more than fear. Anxiety is a full-body experience that affects your thoughts, emotions, nervous system, and even the way you interpret your spiritual life. To heal anxiety, we must begin by understanding what it truly is and what it is not. Many Christians wrestle with anxiety because we are often taught to view it only through a spiritual lens. However, anxiety is a complex and multidimensional response that God Himself designed into the human body as a survival mechanism.Before we can conquer anxiety, we must understand it.

Most people do not realize that anxiety is not a single emotion but an entire system of responses activated within the body. When anxiety rises, it is not because someone is failing spiritually or losing control. It is because the body is doing exactly what it was designed to do in moments of threat. Understanding this truth is liberating for many believers who have spent years feeling ashamed. When you realize that anxiety is not a spiritual defect but a physiological response, you can begin approaching healing with understanding rather than condemnation.

Anxiety is your body's natural alarm system. It activates whenever your brain perceives danger, even if that danger is not actually real. The moment anxiety is triggered, several intricate processes begin inside the body. The first is the firing of the amygdala, the region of the brain responsible for detecting threats. The amygdala was created with one foundational assignment: detect danger and keep you alive. Yet it cannot distinguish between a genuine threat and an emotional memory. It reacts the same way whether you face a physical danger, recall a moment of rejection, anticipate a difficult conversation, or feel uncertain about the future. To the brain, emotional pain can feel as real as physical harm. When the amygdala sounds the alarm, your nervous system immediately shifts into what is commonly known as the fight or flight response. This is the sympathetic nervous system springing into action to protect you. As this happens, your heart rate rises, your breathing becomes shallow, your muscles tighten, your thoughts speed up, and your digestion slows. Your entire body becomes hyper-alert, scanning for danger, bracing for something to go wrong, or preparing you to run, fight, or freeze. This response is not evidence that something is wrong with you spiritually. It is simply biology. God designed your nervous system to respond this way so that you could survive danger.

The amygdala releases cortisol, the body's primary stress hormone. Cortisol in small amounts is helpful and necessary. It keeps you awake, alert, and ready to respond. However, in seasons of chronic anxiety, cortisol becomes overwhelming. Elevated cortisol can lead to irritability, exhaustion, difficulty sleeping, mental fog, emotional strain, and a persistent sense of being on edge. These are physiological responses occurring inside a human body that God created with extraordinary complexity.

Many Christians find themselves trapped in a cycle of shame because of anxiety. They believe that if their faith was stronger, they would not feel the way they do. They imagine that God must be disappointed in them for struggling. They conclude that something must be wrong with them spiritually. Yet shame does not heal anxiety. Shame intensifies it. The truth is that a person can trust God with their whole heart and still experience anxiety in their body. This is because faith and physiology are not enemies. God never intended us to separate what He designed to work together. When we divide them, we place pressure on ourselves that God never commanded us to carry.

Many believers have secretly wrestled for years with the sense that something is wrong with them. They have prayed, fasted, worshiped, and sought deliverance, yet the anxiety persisted. This often leads to confusion and discouragement. The truth is that prayer and worship are powerful, but they are not meant to replace the work of understanding and caring for the mind and body. Scripture shows again and again that God ministers to the whole person. He does not separate the spiritual from the emotional or the physical. He created them to operate in harmony.

One of the most quoted Scriptures regarding anxiety is Philippians 4:6–7, which says, *"Be anxious for nothing, but in everything by prayer and supplication, with thanksgiving, let your requests be made known to God."*

Many interpret this passage as a command to stop feeling anxious, as if Paul were telling believers that anxiety is always a failure of faith. Yet Paul was not condemning believers. He was comforting them. He was not saying that anxiety should never be felt. He was saying that when anxiety does come, there is a place to bring it. Then Paul gives a promise that is both spiritual and neurological. He writes that the peace of God, which surpasses all understanding, will guard your heart and mind in Christ Jesus. The word guard is a military term that describes a soldier standing watch. In other words, God will stand guard over your mind when your mind cannot guard itself. Peace is not something you force. Peace is something God gives as you learn to regulate your inner world and release your fears into His hands.

This Scripture does not shame the anxious believer. It offers them a picture of divine protection. It reminds us that God is willing to step into the places where our bodies and minds feel overwhelmed. His promise is a peace that surpasses understanding, which means it transcends what the nervous system is currently experiencing. It is not a peace you must produce. It is a peace God brings as you learn to breathe, slow your thoughts, process your emotions, and allow His presence to steady you.

True healing from anxiety requires the integration of both faith and science. Science explains how anxiety works in the brain and body. Scripture explains why peace is possible and how God meets us in the middle of our distress. The two together form a complete picture of healing. Scripture soothes the soul and helps rewire the brain. Prayer calms the nervous system. Truth confronts and dismantles the lies that anxiety whispers. Emotional processing allows the brain to release stored trauma. Community restores a sense of safety and belonging, which the nervous system desperately needs. Because anxiety does not originate from one source, it also does not have one single solution. The journey toward healing is layered, gradual, and deeply personal.

When believers begin to understand this, healing becomes a journey rather than a pressure. And the believer discovers that their faith is strengthened when truth and knowledge are allowed to work together.

The good news is that you were fearfully and wonderfully made, both internally and externally. Your thoughts, your emotions, your brain, your body, and your spiritual life are interconnected. God intends to bring healing to every part of you. He invites you into a life where your faith strengthens your mind, your mind supports your emotions, and your emotions no longer control your life. Anxiety does not have the final word. God does, and His word over you is peace, healing, and wholeness.

Chapter 4

The Miracle in the Tool

For much of my life I believed that if something was spiritual, then God alone should handle it. I believed that if victory came from heaven, then heaven would provide it without the need for anything natural. I saw prayer and spiritual authority as the only acceptable methods of breakthrough. But as I grew older, and especially as I walked through my own battle with anxiety, I began to realize something I had overlooked in Scripture for years. Everything is spiritual, yes, but God often chooses to work through methods, people, wisdom, and tools. The supernatural and the natural were never meant to compete. They were meant to cooperate. What we place in God's hands becomes the vessel through which His power flows.

When David stepped onto the battlefield to face Goliath, Scripture tells us he came *"in the name of the Lord of hosts"* (1 Samuel 17:45). His confidence was not in the sling. His faith was not in his aim. His hope rested fully in God. Yet David still bent down, picked up five smooth stones, and used the sling he had practiced with for years. God could have dropped Goliath with a breath. He could have sent an angel to strike the giant. But instead He chose to use the tool in David's hand. The miracle was God's. The sling belonged to David.

Moses experienced the same pattern. When God called him to lead Israel out of Egypt, Moses stood there with nothing but a shepherd's staff. Yet God asked him, *"What is that in your hand?"* and Moses answered, "A staff" (Exodus 4:2). That ordinary piece of wood became the instrument through which seas parted, water flowed from rocks, plagues were stopped, and nations were judged. God could have split the Red Sea without Moses lifting a thing, yet He commanded Moses to stretch out the staff so heaven's power could flow through it.

Elijah understood this as well. When he encountered the widow at Zarephath, God could have dropped bread from heaven as He did in the wilderness, yet Elijah asked her to bring what she had. *"Bring me a morsel of bread"* (1 Kings 17:11). She only had a little flour and a little oil, but God multiplied it because she offered it. The miracle was supernatural, but the means were natural.

Another powerful example is Peter and the empty nets. After a night of catching nothing, Jesus told him, *"Launch out into the deep and let down your nets for a catch"* (Luke

5:4). When Peter obeyed and lowered the nets on the other side, Scripture says, *"they caught a great number of fish, and their net was breaking"* (Luke 5:6). Jesus could have filled the boat without Peter touching a rope. But He used Peter's boat, Peter's nets, and Peter's obedience. The miracle came through the tool Peter already possessed.

Even Jesus used tools and methods when performing miracles. When feeding the multitudes, He did not create food out of thin air. Instead He took the lunch of a small boy. *"He blessed and broke them, and gave them to the disciples"* (Luke 9:16). Five loaves and two fish became more than enough. When healing a blind man, Jesus made mud with His hands, placed it on the man's eyes, and instructed him to wash in the pool of Siloam. *"So he went and washed, and came back seeing"* (John 9:7). Jesus could have restored his sight instantly with a word, which he did in many other occasions. Yet He also used mud, water, movement, and obedience.

Now I understand that these were also acts of faith. I am not discounting that. Their obedience was faith. Their trust in God was faith. But the point I am trying to make is that God used tools. He worked through what they had. He chose to include natural means as part of supernatural moments. Their faith activated the miracle, but the tools became the vessels through which the miracle flowed.

Scripture is full of this pattern. God provided for the widow through Elisha by multiplying the oil she poured into borrowed jars. *"Go, borrow vessels from everywhere"* (2 Kings 4:3). The size of her miracle was determined by the number of jars she gathered. The jars were natural. The oil was supernatural.

When Naaman sought healing from leprosy, Elisha did not wave his hand dramatically. Instead he instructed Naaman to wash seven times in the Jordan River. *"So he went down and dipped seven times in the Jordan... and his flesh was restored"* (2 Kings 5:14). The water had no power. The obedience did. When Joshua led Israel across the Jordan River, the waters did not part until the priests carrying the ark *"stepped into the edge of the water"* (Joshua 3:15). God waited for their feet to touch the river before the miracle began.

Just as God uses practical tools throughout scripture, He also uses spiritual tools we already treasure. Prayer is a tool. Reading Scripture is a tool. Worship is a tool. Reflection is a tool. But God also uses tools that many believers overlook. Journaling can become a tool that helps uncover buried emotions. A trusted therapist can become a tool that helps untangle trauma. A counselor can become a tool that helps you give language to pain you have carried for decades. These tools do not make your healing less spiritual. They reveal the many ways God meets His people.

This truth reshaped my understanding of healing, especially emotional and mental healing. For years I believed that if something was spiritual, then only spiritual methods would be needed. But Scripture shows us that God frequently uses natural tools as part of His supernatural deliverance. In the same way, when our mental health is affected, God is able to heal us through prayer alone. However, there are times when therapy becomes a tool. Counseling becomes a tool. Medication becomes a stabilizing tool. Support groups, community, wisdom, rest, boundaries, and even learning new coping skills become tools. These do not replace God's ability. They complement it. They create space for restoration to take root.

In my later chapters we will talk about some of the tools God allows us to use, tools that help us heal mentally, emotionally, and spiritually. These tools do not replace the hand of God. They simply work in harmony with it. They allow His wisdom to take shape in practical ways, and they honor the truth that faith is not the absence of action but the courage to cooperate with God's leading.

Faith does not mean refusing tools. Faith means trusting God enough to use them. David still had to swing the sling. Moses still had to raise the staff. The widow still had to offer the flour. The disciples still had to pass the bread. The blind man still had to wash the mud. Peter still had to throw the nets. Naaman still had to dip in the water. The priests still had to step into the river. Tools are not the absence of faith.

Tools are often the expression of it.

When we embrace both the spiritual and the practical, we begin to experience the full spectrum of God's healing. He moves through prayer. He moves through Scripture. He moves through His Spirit. And He also moves through the tools He places in our hands.

If God could use a sling, a staff, oil jars, water, mud, loaves and obedience, then surely He can use therapy, counselors, community, journaling, and wise medical care today. Your healing is still spiritual. Your progress is still sacred. Your journey is still filled with God's presence. Nothing is wasted. Nothing is random. Everything can become a tool in the hands of a God who heals.

Chapter 5

Overwhelmed

I remember times when I felt completely overwhelmed, like everything was closing in at once and I could not slow my thoughts down or catch my breath. Even small things felt heavy, and decisions that should have been simple felt impossible. It was not just stress. It felt like something deeper, something that touched my mind, my body, and even my faith.

Anxiety often feels larger than anything else in your life. It can rise suddenly, speak louder than truth, and overwhelm you even when you believe deeply in God's promises. Many believers wrestle with the same question: Why does anxiety feel so powerful, so immediate, and so difficult to quiet? To understand this, you must first understand what anxiety actually is. Anxiety is not just an emotion. It is an entire internal system involving your brain, your nervous system, your body chemistry, your past experiences, your capacity for stress, and your spiritual sensitivity. Anxiety involves your whole being, which is why it can feel so consuming.

And because anxiety engages the whole person, the experience can feel like standing under a sudden wave that you never saw coming. One moment you seem fine, managing your responsibilities, navigating your day, and even feeling spiritually strong. Then the next moment your mind fixates on a single fear that refuses to let go. It's times like this that often leave you wondering why anxiety feels so disproportionate to the situation and why it seems to bypass faith so quickly. But the truth is that anxiety is not fighting against your faith. Anxiety many times is just responding to your biology.

To understand this more clearly, we look to one of the most profound biblical pictures of emotional distress: Jesus in the Garden of Gethsemane. On the night before the crucifixion, Jesus carried the weight of the world on His shoulders. He knew what was coming. He understood the pain He would endure. He was fully God, yet He faced the moment with the full emotional experience of a human being. Scripture says, "My soul is exceedingly sorrowful, even unto death" (Matthew 26:38). This was not just a feeling He was having. It was a crushing emotional pressure, the kind of weight that presses into the deepest parts of the human spirit.

This statement reveals that Jesus experienced a depth of emotional agony that felt so overwhelming it brought Him to the edge of His physical limits. His words describe emotional pain so intense it felt as though life itself was slipping away. This does not diminish His divinity; it displays His full humanity. It also teaches us that when we are feeling emotional overwhelmed we are only human. Anxiety in the body is a sign of being human.

Luke describes the moment with even more vivid detail. He writes that Jesus was in such anguish that "His sweat became like great drops of blood falling down to the ground" (Luke 22:44). This phenomenon, known today as hematidrosis, occurs only under extreme stress. This means Jesus was not simply worried. He was overwhelmed. His body responded as any human body would under intense emotional strain. His heart raced. His muscles tightened. His mind carried the heaviness of what lay ahead. And yet Jesus was the Son of God. His distress was not weakness, or spiritual failure. His experience in the garden shows us that deep anxiety can occur even in perfect obedience.

This moment in Gethsemane teaches us something crucial: Anxiety means you are human. It means you feel deeply. It means you carry responsibilities, memories, expectations, and fears that matter to you. Jesus's experience affirms that emotional intensity is part of the human condition. He prayed, "Father, if You are willing, remove this cup from Me. Nevertheless, not My will, but Yours be done" (Luke 22:42). Jesus did not hide His distress. He brought it into the presence of

God.

The word agony in the greek is the word agonia which is translated severe mental struggles and emotions. There is a profound truth in this passage. Jesus was in deep agony and sweat drops of blood. the good news is this. Before Jesus shed his blood for your sin, He sweat his blood for you anxiety. Amen! that's good news.

Scripture says *"The truth makes your free" John 8:32 (KNJV)*. And that is where healing truly begins. Not in pretending. Not in suppressing. Not in acting as though you do not feel what you feel. Healing begins where honesty begins. Jesus shows us that He was transparent before His Father. He teaches us that it is possible to feel emotional anguish and still trust God entirely.

Anxiety feels overwhelming partly because your body is designed to respond to perceived threats with urgency. The amygdala, the alarm center of your brain, reacts instantly to anything that resembles danger. It cannot distinguish between a real threat and an emotional one.

The CU Boulder Study (2018): Published in the journal *Neuron*, researchers at the **University of Colorado Boulder** found that imagining a threat lights up the same regions of the brain (like the auditory cortex, amygdala, and ventromedial prefrontal cortex) as physically experiencing it. The study concluded that statistically, real and imagined exposure to a threat yield incredibly similar responses at the whole-brain level.

To your nervous system, a painful memory, a conversation you dread, an unexpected change, or the possibility of rejection can feel as threatening as physical harm. The fight or flight response activates. Your heart beats faster. Your breathing shifts. Your thoughts accelerate. Your body readies itself to survive.

This is why anxiety seems to come out of nowhere. The amygdala fires before the rational part of your brain processes what is happening. Your body reacts first. Understanding this helps believers release the shame that often accompanies anxiety. What you are experiencing is how the mechanics of a brain are designed to protect you.

Jesus experienced the human version of that same intensity in the garden. He felt the weight before the event took place. His body responded to what His spirit understood. This is why anxiety feels so sudden and powerful. It is tied to the way God created the human body. Anxiety comes quickly because biology reacts before the rational part of the brain has time to interpret what is happening. You may know you are safe, yet your body may still act as if danger is near.

Jesus also shows us why anxiety lingers. When you face something overwhelming, your mind rehearses it. Your thoughts return to it. Your body does not forget the sensation of fear. In the garden, Jesus prayed multiple times. Scripture says, "He went away again and prayed a third time, saying the same words" (Matthew 26:44). His repeated prayer reveals a powerful truth: emotional weight is rarely lifted instantly. Even Jesus returned to the same place of surrender more than once. Anxiety often calls for repeated moments of grounding, repeated moments of surrender, repeated moments of returning to God. Emotions often release in layers. Fear often loosens slowly. The mind often calms gradually.

Jesus shows us that bringing anxiety to God repeatedly is obedience. Gethsemane is not just a place of agony. It is also a place of assurance. An angel appeared to Jesus and strengthened Him, reminding us that in moments of intense distress, God does not leave us alone. His presence does not always remove the weight immediately, but it gives us the strength to endure it. In your own moments of anxiety, God offers the same nearness, the same strengthening, the same compassion. He understands your physiology, your emotions, and your limitations. He created every part of you.

Philippians 4:6-7 says, *Be anxious for nothing, but in everything by prayer and supplication, with thanksgiving, let your requests be made known to God; and the peace of God, which surpasses all understanding, will guard your hearts and minds through Christ Jesus.*

Did you notice that in this verse it does not say that after situation changes then we can have the peace of God. No, It states that if we bring our situation to God, He will give us peace in the midst of it.

Anxiety feels overwhelming because it touches all of you at once. It affects the mind, the body, the emotions, and the spirit. Yet the story of Jesus in the garden reminds us that it is a moment where faith must meet reality. Anxiety does not separate you from God. It reveals your need for His presence, His strength, and His peace. The garden teaches us that overwhelming moments are not the end of your story. They are the places where God meets you, strengthens you, and prepares you for victory.

Chapter 6

The Science of Anxiety

Let's talk about the brain for a moment. As I shared in chapter 2, anxiety is not simply a feeling. It is a biological event. It is an intricate sequence of reactions involving the brain, nervous system, hormones, memory, and even your immune system.

When you understand what is happening inside you, the fear surrounding anxiety begins to lose its power. You realize anxiety is not a character flaw. It is a physical system that has become overwhelmed. And the more we learn about this system, the more compassion we gain for ourselves and for those who struggle.

Anxiety begins in the brain, but not in the part of the brain where rational thought occurs. It begins in the limbic system, the emotional center. The limbic system contains the amygdala, the hippocampus, and the hypothalamus. These structures work together to keep you alive by detecting danger and responding quickly. Their priority is survival, not logic. This is why anxiety often feels irrational. The limbic system reacts before the reasoning part of your brain has time to interpret what is happening.

Let's talk about how the brain works once again. As I said before, the amygdala is the alarm. Its job is to detect threat and activate the body's emergency response. When the amygdala senses anything resembling danger, it sends an urgent message through the hypothalamus to the rest of the nervous system. This message triggers the release of adrenaline, which increases heart rate, forces your breathing to speed up, and prepares your muscles to move. This reaction is automatic. You cannot pray it away in the moment, nor can you think it away instantly. Your body responds before you can consciously intervene.

The hippocampus is the memory keeper in the brain. It stores emotional memories, especially those connected to fear or trauma. If the hippocampus detects something similar to a past hurt, even if it is only a tone of voice or a facial expression, it alerts the amygdala. This means your body can react to echoes of old wounds as if they are happening now. This is one reason trauma survivors experience anxiety even when life appears peaceful. The body is responding to a memory, not a moment.

The prefrontal cortex, the part of your brain responsible for logic, reasoning, and decision-making, is the last one to receive the signal. By the time it begins to evaluate whether the danger is real, the amygdala has already sent the body into high alert. This explains why people experiencing anxiety often say, "I know I am safe, but I do not feel safe." The amygdala speaks first. Logic speaks last.

These brain structures activate the autonomic nervous system, which has two main branches. The sympathetic nervous system is the accelerator. It prepares you for fight or flight. The parasympathetic nervous system is the brake. It brings you back to a calm state. Anxiety becomes chronic when the accelerator stays pressed down and the brake becomes weak or unresponsive. Over time, the body forgets how to return to rest.

Cortisol, the body's primary stress hormone, plays a significant role in this cycle. Cortisol is released to help you cope with danger. In short bursts it is helpful. But when cortisol levels remain high for extended periods, it affects every major system in the body. It disrupts sleep. It weakens the immune system. It impacts digestion. It affects mood, concentration, memory, and emotional regulation. Cortisol also shrinks the hippocampus over time, making emotional memories more reactive and increasing the likelihood of anxiety. In other words, long-term stress changes the brain.

Another dimension of anxiety involves the vagus nerve. The vagus nerve is the longest cranial nerve. As the primary driver of the parasympathetic ("rest and digest") nervous system, it acts as a bidirectional communication highway between your brain, heart, lungs, digestive system, and other organs. It helps regulate your body's organs.

When the vagus nerve is strong, your body can recover quickly from stress. When it is weak, stress lingers. Trauma, chronic fear, and emotional neglect can weaken the vagus nerve, making it harder to shift out of anxiety. Strengthening the vagus nerve is part of healing and explains why breathing techniques, prayer, worship, and grounding exercises are so effective. They activate the parasympathetic nervous system and signal safety to the brain.

Somatic memory, the body's memory, is another important factor. The body stores experiences, especially those involving fear, shame, abandonment, or sudden loss. Muscles carry tension. The chest carries fear. The stomach carries dread. The nervous system carries patterns. Emotional experiences that were never fully processed stay trapped in the body. This is why some people cry unexpectedly, feel panic without a trigger, or experience physical symptoms without medical explanation. The body is speaking the language of unprocessed pain.

David understood this experience emotionally long before science explained it physically. In Psalm 32 he wrote, *"When I kept silent, my bones wasted away through my groaning all day long"* He was describing the physical toll of unprocessed emotion. His body carried the weight of what his heart tried to hide. Again in Psalms he wrote, *"My heart throbs, my strength fails me"* (Psalm 38:10), revealing how deeply emotional turmoil affected him physically.

Modern science now confirms that emotional suffering is stored not only in the mind but also in the body. What David described poetically, neuroscience now describes biologically. Emotional pain becomes physical pain. Unspoken sorrow becomes tightness in the chest. Unresolved fear becomes a racing heart. Stress that is never processed becomes illness in the body.

The Book of Psalmist shows us the humanity of a man who felt anxiety in his bones, and science shows us why.

The most hopeful part of this science is the concept of neuroplasticity. Neuroplasticity means the brain can change.

Pathways formed in trauma can be rewired. Patterns of fear can be replaced with patterns of safety. The nervous system can learn to relax again. The body can learn what peace feels like. Healing is not only possible. It is biological. It is built into the way God designed the human brain. You are not stuck. You are not broken beyond repair. The systems that formed anxiety can also form healing.

Understanding the science behind anxiety is important. It brings clarity. It reveals the remarkable way God designed the body and mind. And it shows that healing is not only spiritual. It is physical. It is emotional. It is neurological. God meets you in all three areas. Healing does not require you to ignore the science. Healing requires you to embrace it and allow God to work through it.

Chapter 7

When the Body Remembers What the Mind Tries to Forget

There is a reason many people are confused by their anxiety. They look at their current circumstances and cannot understand why they feel overwhelmed, panicked, or emotionally flooded. They assume the pressure of today is the cause, when in reality, today is only the trigger. The body responds to what the mind has tried to forget. The mind learns how to silence memories, bury pain, and rewrite the narrative in order to function. But the body keeps its own record. It stores every wound, every fear, every moment of pressure, every heartbreak, every abandonment, and every trauma as if it happened yesterday. The body remembers even when the mind insists it has moved on.

When my granddaughter graduated from kindergarten,

our whole family came to celebrate and show our support. As we were leaving, I was holding hands with my two granddaughters, one six years old and the other four. Suddenly, my eighty-year-old mother-in-law stepped off the curb, lost her footing, and fell hard to the ground. She hit her face and immediately began bleeding from her mouth and nose.

Everyone rushed to help. Family members were alarmed, people began gathering around her, and the school nurse quickly came over to provide care. As I looked at my two granddaughters, I could see fear in their eyes. They were trying to make sense of what they were seeing.

I gently led them away from the scene. It wasn't because I was unconcerned about my mother-in-law. I was deeply concerned. I simply recognized that children process traumatic events differently than adults. I know I cannot protect my grandchildren from every difficult experience in life. Pain, loss, disappointment, and unexpected events are part of life. But I also understand that every significant emotional experience plants a seed. Some seeds produce strength, courage, and resilience. Others can produce fear, anxiety, and insecurity if they are not properly understood and processed.

My goal was not to shield them from reality but to help guard their hearts. Children are constantly learning from what they see, hear, and experience. At that moment, I felt it was wise to remove them from the intensity of the situation until they could better understand what was happening.

The truth is that those seeds do not disappear simply because time passes. Experiences, especially painful ones, have a way of lodging themselves deep within us. What is planted in childhood often continues to influence us long into adulthood. Many people assume they have moved on because they no longer think about a particular event, but healing and forgetting are not the same thing.

This is why emotions often feel disproportionate to the moment. This is why people say, "I should be fine. Nothing major is happening." Yet their anxiety rises, their anger flares, or their fear takes over. The body is not reacting only to the present. It is reacting to the past. It is responding to wounds the mind decided were too painful to revisit. The mind wants to forget, but the body refuses to let go. When life becomes stressful, when pressure builds, and when exhaustion piles up, the body begins to speak loudly. It cries out for the healing the mind has avoided.

One of the most overlooked realities is that pain and trauma are sticky. They cling to the soul like tar. Even when you think you have moved on, the residue often remains. Then when a new pain enters your life, the fresh wound pulls the old wounds to the surface. A betrayal today may awaken abandonment from childhood. A stressful season at work may stir memories of past instability. A conflict in the present can reach backward and drag forgotten experiences into full view. Trauma is not just about what happened to you. It is about what attached itself to you.

This is why healing matters. If wounds are not properly addressed, the seeds they plant continue to produce fruit long after the original event is over. What began as a moment becomes a mindset. What started as a wound becomes a stronghold. What was once an experience becomes an identity. Yet God never intended for us to live bound to the pain of our past. He desires to heal the wounds, remove the residue, and free us from the burdens we were never meant to carry. I will share more about this in a later chapter, because this truth has shaped far more of our lives than most of us realize.

I did not understand any of this until much later in life. For years, I lived convinced that my childhood no longer affected me. I believed that if I worked hard enough, pushed long enough, and stayed focused on what was ahead, the past would lose its grip. I convinced myself of this. And like many people who grow up with instability, trauma, or fear, I learned how to keep going. What I did not realize was that the little boy inside me was still hurting. That the wounds of my childhood were still waiting to be healed. I simply kept moving because slowing down meant feeling what I had worked my whole life to avoid.

As I grew older, I tried to outrun the pain. I buried myself in work. When work was not enough, I buried myself in ministry. Ministry became my refuge, my identity, my safe place, and my hiding place. As long as I poured myself out for others, I did not have to face the places in me that had never healed. I could encourage broken people while ignoring my own brokenness. I could preach about restoration while avoiding the exact rooms in my soul where restoration was needed. And I told myself that as long as I was helping others, I was fine.

But the body does not forget. And when the body can no longer carry what the mind refuses to face, it speaks. It speaks through anxiety. It speaks through panic. It speaks through sleepless nights. It speaks through spiraling thoughts. It speaks through physical symptoms doctors cannot explain. That is what happened to me. Anxiety struck me with a force I never expected. It was as if the buried wounds of my entire life rose all at once, demanding to be acknowledged. What felt sudden was actually decades of stored pain crashing through the walls I had built around my heart.

There were nights when fear pressed so heavily on me that I wondered if I would make it through. My mind spiraled and panic swept over me like a wave I could not outrun. And in the darkest moments, when my thoughts drifted into places I never imagined they would, I realized I was not fighting something new. I was fighting everything I had never healed.

My wife walked through this valley with me. She stayed awake when I could not sleep. She prayed when I could not pray. She cried when the weight became too much. She once told me she could feel the fear in the room, like something thick in the air. It frightened her, and it frightened me. These were the moments when I realized that my body had remembered what my mind had tried to forget.

It was in this season I discovered a truth no one had ever taught me. When the mind refuses to deal with pain, the body will force the conversation. If you do not face your traumas, eventually what once affected you will rise to the surface and demand healing. My anxiety was a sign of a wounded soul.

I see this truth woven all throughout Scripture. The Bible is filled with people whose bodies carried the weight of memories their minds wanted to avoid. The prophet Jeremiah wrote, *"My soul remembers and sinks within me"* (Lamentations 3:20). His soul remembered even when his mind wished it did not. Yet he followed it with, *"But this I call to mind, and therefore I have hope"* (Lamentations 3:21). Healing began when he stopped denying the memories that surfaced.

We also see this in the life of Job. After suffering unimaginable loss, Job cried out, *"The arrows of the Almighty are in me; my spirit drinks their poison"* (Job 6:4). Job was not simply reacting to his current pain. His body was responding to layers of grief, fear, and devastation that had accumulated over time. His cry was deep because his wounds were deep.

But one of the most powerful examples is the man at the pool of Bethesda in John 5. For thirty-eight years he lived with paralysis, but what truly held him was not only physical infirmity but the emotional memory of disappointment. He had watched others step ahead of him. He believed healing was possible for everyone except him. His body carried the weight of decades of hopelessness. When Jesus approached him, He asked, *"Do you want to be made well?"* (John 5:6). It was not just a question about his legs. It was a question about his heart. Jesus touched the memory before He touched the muscle. Christ healed the part of the man that suffered long before his body stopped working.

This is how God heals wounded souls. He meets us in the places where the pain has been stored. He meets us where the body remembers what the mind has tried to forget. He meets us in the memories we buried, in the emotions we silenced, in the stories we ran from, and in the wounds we never acknowledged.

My journey has taught me that anxiety is often a sign that something hidden is ready to be healed. It is how the body calls for restoration. It is the heart asking to be heard. And it is the grace of God inviting you to stop running, stop burying, and stop pretending the past no longer matters. Healing begins when honesty begins. Healing begins when the mind finally agrees to listen to what the body has been trying to say. Healing begins when you allow God into the places you closed long ago.

Anxiety may feel like a breaking, but often it is the beginning of restoration. It is your invitation. It is God saying the time has come for the memories to heal, the wounds to close, the soul to rest, and the body to finally let go of what it has carried for far too long.

Chapter 8

Rewrite the Story

One of the most exhausting realities of anxiety is the way the mind creates scenes that never happened. You can be sitting in a quiet room, surrounded by calm, and still feel your heart racing as if danger is closing in. You can be driving down a familiar road or lying in bed at night, and suddenly your thoughts begin spiraling into fear. Your breathing changes. Your stomach tightens. Your body responds to a threat that does not exist.

The fear is not coming from your surroundings. It is coming from a story your mind has written about a future that has not happened. In moments like these, the words of Jesus whisper back to us, *"Do not worry about tomorrow"* (Matthew 6:34). But when anxiety is triggered, the mind tries to convince you that tomorrow is already collapsing.

There was a time in my life when I did not understand this. I believed every thought my mind produced, letting each one consume me. I treated every worst-case scenario as unquestionable truth. My mind could take the smallest concern and turn it into a full-blown crisis.

It felt like my brain had become a director producing a psychological thriller. I worried about things that had not happened. I worried about things that were unlikely to happen. I even worried about things that were impossible to happen. The scenes were so vivid they felt real, and my body reacted as if they were. In those moments, the promise, *"You keep him in perfect peace whose mind is stayed on You"* (Isaiah 26:3), felt so far away, even though it was the truth I desperately needed.

Some nights I would wake up with my heart pounding, convinced something terrible was unfolding. I could be sitting at dinner, trying to relax, and suddenly imagine a hard conversation that had never occurred or a crisis that did not exist. I would walk into church with a smile on my face, while inside my mind replayed scenes of failure, conflict, or disappointment. I found myself constantly asking my wife if everything was okay. I was fighting battles that were not real, yet they drained my strength as if they were.

This is the power of catastrophic thinking. The mind writes stories and the body reacts to them. The nervous system cannot tell the difference between imagination and reality. It reacts to what you picture as if you are living through it. Your body prepares for danger even when there is none. The Scripture, *"Be still, and know that I am God"* (Psalm 46:10), becomes both an invitation and a challenge, because stillness is difficult when the mind is loud.

Elijah experienced something deeply familiar to anyone who has battled anxiety. After one of Scripture's greatest victories, Elijah suddenly found himself overwhelmed with fear. The threat against him was real, but the fear inside him became larger than reality. Fear magnified the danger. Fear wrote a story. Fear convinced him that the worst was inevitable. Scripture says Elijah ran into the wilderness, collapsed under a broom tree, and said, *"It is enough. Now, Lord, take my life"* (1 Kings 19:4).

This was what happens when fear creates a future so dark that you cannot see a way through it. Elijah believed a storyline that anxiety had written. His imagination convinced him that he was done, that his life was over, and that nothing good lay ahead. He went even deeper into isolation, hiding in a cave, not because his calling had ended, but because he believed the lie that he was completely alone. He said, *"I alone am left, and they seek to take my life"* (1 Kings 19:10). But Elijah was not alone. The God who later declared, *"I will never leave you nor forsake you"* (Hebrews 13:5), was standing right there.

This is what catastrophic thinking does. It convinces you that you are alone when you are not. It convinces you that everything is falling apart when it is not. It convinces you that danger is certain when it is not. It turns a moment of fear into a script that feels impossible to escape. Anxiety takes a single thought and writes an entire story of disaster.

I know exactly what that feels like. I have been in my own cave, believing my own thoughts more than God's truth. I have imagined endings that never came. I have feared outcomes that never materialized. I have rehearsed conversations that never happened. I have carried stress that existed only in the world my mind created. Anxiety convinced me that something was wrong with me spiritually, that I was alone in what I felt, and that I was heading toward disaster.

Just like Elijah, the story I believed was not true. I was not alone. I was not abandoned. I was not beyond help. I was living inside a narrative that anxiety had written instead of the truth God was speaking.

Healing did not begin when my fear disappeared. Healing began when I recognized the story fear wrote. Healing began when I realized I could rewrite the story. Healing began when I stopped accepting every anxious thought as truth. I started clinging to the promises of God.

God did not ask Elijah, "What is wrong with you." He asked, *"What are you doing here"* (1 Kings 19:9). Not as a rebuke, but as an invitation. An invitation out of the cave. Out of the imagined future. Out of the storyline of fear. Out of the movie playing inside his mind. God met Elijah where he was, then led him into truth. This is the same God who says, *"The Lord is near to the brokenhearted"* (Psalm 34:18), and near to the anxious, even when we cannot feel Him.

When I was going through this my wife Heather would constantly remind me to rewrite the story. So that is what I started doing. Everytime a story of doom and gloom would pop into my mind. I would stop and start rewriting the story. I started putting faith ending and adding the truth of God's Word into the story. Your mind may write terrifying scenes. Your fear may tell you you are alone. Your imagination may show you disaster and tell you it's over. But you have the ability to rewrite the story.

In faith I began to rewrite the stories in my head. instead of seeing the worst case scenario I would change it to a happy faith filled ending.

I discovered that I did not have to follow every story my mind created. You do not have to believe every prediction your fear imagines. You do not have to live inside the movie your anxiety is directing. You can interrupt the script. You can speak truth and rewrite the story.

Healing begins when you stop believing the story fear wrote and start rewriting the story God is telling. With every truth you speak, with every anxious thought you interrupt, you are reclaiming another piece of your peace.

Chapter 9

The Wounded Soul

During one of the darkest seasons of my life, I was battling a deep depression. I felt heavy, tired in my soul, and spiritually drained. My wife was speaking at a women's conference in the High Desert, and I went with her simply to be present and supportive.

During worship, something inside me began to stir. I felt overwhelmed, like everything I had been carrying for months was rising to the surface all at once. I tried to hold it together, standing there, hands raised, doing what I had done so many times before in church settings. But this time it felt different. I wasn't leading. I wasn't ministering. I was barely holding on.

That's when I noticed a fellow pastor friend of mine walk into the room. His wife was also one of the speakers. We had known each other for years. When he came into the room, he walked over and stood beside me and began to worship. I'm sure he could sense something was off. After a few minutes, he placed his hand on my shoulder. The moment he did, something broke. I began to weep uncontrollably. It was as if everything I had held inside finally came rushing out. He didn't draw attention. When he saw my emotional state, he quietly guided me to the back of the room. We knelt down together and he put his arms around me. He held me like a father holding a hurting child. I cried into his shoulder and couldn't stop. The pain, the exhaustion, the confusion, the pressure of ministry, the weight I had been carrying in silence, it all poured out.

After some time, when the sobbing slowed, he looked at me with a seriousness I'll never forget.

He said, "Tom… you have a wounded soul."

I had never heard those words before. Not "you're tired." Not "you're stressed." Not "you're burned out." A wounded soul.

In that moment, I knew what he was saying was true. Something inside me had been injured. My spirit had been worn down by the weight of stress, disappointments and past traumas that I had never taken time to heal from.

That moment became a turning point. For the first time, I realized I didn't just need rest. I needed healing. I needed God to tend to what had been broken within me. And it took a brother, a pastor, a man sensitive to the Spirit of God, to help me see what I had been unable to see for myself.

"You have a wounded soul."

That realization became the beginning of restoration.

One of the most overlooked realities in the life of a believer is the condition of the soul. Scripture teaches that we are body, soul, and spirit, and each part carries its own needs, its own vulnerabilities, and its own responses to life.

The soul is the place of emotions, memories, wounds, and identity. It is where we feel joy, but also where we feel grief. It is where we experience love, but also where we carry heartbreak. And when the soul becomes wounded, everything else in life is affected.

A wounded soul can sometimes it looks like irritability, withdrawal, or unexplained sadness. Sometimes it looks like perfectionism, overworking, or avoiding deep relationships. Sometimes it looks like anxiety that rises without warning.

A wounded soul remembers things the mind has tried to forget. It holds the echoes of old betrayals, losses, abandonment, rejection, and moments when life broke something inside that never fully healed. Even when a person feels spiritually strong, their soul can still be limping quietly under the weight of experiences they never processed.

I know this because my soul carried wounds from the past. My early years were marked by layers of pain I tried to bury. I walked through rejection that shaped the way I saw myself. I endured the trauma of losing my father and two brothers, losses so heavy that grief settled into the deepest parts of me.

I carried the hidden shame of being molested, a wound I locked away in silence because I did not know how to process something so devastating. These were an accumulation of past pain that formed a kind of inner limp.

At seventeen, I surrendered my life to Christ, and it felt like hope finally broke through the cracks. I was excited about this new life in Christ. I ran into ministry with everything I had, believing that if I stayed busy for the Lord, I could outrun my brokenness. I thought serving would silence the ache. I assumed pouring into others would heal what I refused to confront.

But the soul does not forget. And eventually everything I buried found its way back to the surface. AS i said before, pain and trauma are sticky like tar. They cling to the soul in ways that time alone cannot dissolve. Even when someone feels they have moved on, even when they believe they have left certain wounds behind, the residue of old pain remains attached to the inner life. So when a new hurt happens, whether it is betrayal, rejection, a fresh loss, or a moment of disappointment, it does not simply create another wound. It pulls the old ones to the surface. New trauma reaches back, grabs unresolved pain, and drags it forward.

A recent conflict can awaken childhood rejection. A painful conversation can stir shame from decades earlier. A new loss can reopen grief that was never fully processed. Tar sticks to tar. Old pain sticks to new pain until the soul is overwhelmed by a mixture of memories and emotions. The soul is not reacting only to what is happening in the present. It is reacting to everything in the past that has happened in that same emotional place.

When the soul is wounded in this way, the enemy will try to exploit it.. He takes advantage of the cracks left by trauma. He speaks lies that cling to old hurts. He uses fear to reinforce patterns of pain. He whispers accusations into unhealed places, hoping to convince the believer that their suffering is their identity. He attempts to distort what God wants to redeem, to cloud what God wants to clarify, and to confuse what God is trying to heal.

But even in these moments, God does not distance Himself. David declared, "He restores my soul," this is not as poetic imagery but a revelation of God's character. God moves toward broken places. He seeks out the parts of the heart that have been torn. He does not ignore wounds, overlook trauma, or ask His children to simply toughen up. He draws near.

The part believers often forget is that God wants to heal your wounded soul. He is not waiting for you to clean yourself up or hold yourself together. Healing is part of His nature. He is a Shepherd who tends to wounds, a Father who comforts His children, a Healer who goes straight to the places that hurt the most. God desires to enter the memories you have tried to bury, and lifts the grief that has lingered. He restores innocence that was stolen. There is no pain too deep, no wound too old, no trauma too tangled for His hands.

This truth echoes through Scripture. Paul writes *"My grace is sufficient for you, for my power is made perfect in weakness."* And then Paul responds to this statement with a declaration that speaks to every wounded soul, *"For when I am weak, then I am strong"* (2 Corinthians 12:9–10). He is saying that weakness is the doorway where God's strength enters the human story. The place were God begins His deepest work.

Many people hesitate bringing their wounds to God, but God wants you to bring it all to Him, so that He could heal you. He wants to bring you to a place where you can live again, love again, trust again, breathe again, and step into the future without dragging yesterday's wounds behind you.

When God heals a soul, He does not do it halfway. His healing is not a temporary fix but a deep restoration. He works layer by layer, gently uncovering the roots of pain and replacing them with His truth. He confronts the enemy's lies. He rewrites shame-filled narratives. He lifts heaviness that has smothered the heart for years. He brings clarity, peace, and a strength that cannot be shaken.

God wants to heal your wounded soul because He knows who you are without the pain. He knows the version of you that trauma tried to bury. He sees the strength beneath the fear, the courage beneath the anxiety, the joy beneath the sorrow. His desire to heal you is rooted in His love and anchored in His covenant. Healing is not just something He can do. It is something He wants to do.

And when you allow God into those wounded places, the soul that once trembled becomes the soul that stands. The soul that once hid becomes the soul that breathes freely. The soul that once felt fragile becomes the soul that testifies of God's faithfulness. Every healed wound becomes a place where His glory rests. Every restored memory becomes a reminder that you are not alone. Every scar becomes proof that God brings beauty out of brokenness.

God does not just restore the soul. He restores the person. He restores the life. He restores everything the enemy tried to steal, diminish, or distort. The healing He offers is transformational. It reaches into the deepest parts of who you are and makes you whole in ways you never imagined.

You are not too damaged for God. You are not too complicated for Him. You are not too far gone. Your wounds do not intimidate Him. Your pain does not push Him away. God wants to heal your wounded soul because He loves you, and He refuses to let brokenness have the final word over your life.

Chapter 10

When the Enemy Whispers and the Soul Trembles

There is a part of the human experience that many believers do not talk about openly. It is the place where spiritual warfare and emotional trauma collide. It is in this area where the enemy's lies mix with the wounds of the heart, creating confusion, fear, and sometimes overwhelming anxiety. This chapter exists because anxiety is rarely simple. It is often multi-layered, complex, and deeply woven into the realities of both the spiritual and human experience. Many believers find themselves facing attacks from the enemy, carrying the scars of past trauma, and wrestling with intense battles in their minds. Sometimes all of these collide at the same time.

Many Christians grow up believing that anxiety is always a spiritual attack. Others believe it's emotional or psychological. But the truth is this: anxiety can be spiritual, emotional, psychological, or a mixture of all three. The Bible teaches that we are body, soul, and spirit. When one of those parts is wounded, the other parts are affected. When the soul is bruised, the body reacts. When the mind carries trauma, the spirit feels the weight. And when the enemy sees that vulnerability, he presses into it with lies, suggestions, accusations, and fear.

Scripture makes it clear that there is an enemy of our soul. Jesus said *"the thief comes only to steal, kill, and destroy"*. Paul said *"we do not wrestle against flesh and blood but against powers and principalities that operate in unseen realms"*. Peter said *"the enemy prowls around like a roaring lion seeking someone to devour"*. The entire story of Scripture shows that the enemy works through deception, intimidation, manipulation, and discouragement. He speaks lies to weaken the believer's confidence, distort their identity, and cloud their view of God.

For many believers, anxiety shows up as a battlefield of the mind. Sometimes the enemy attacks through fear, intrusive thoughts, overwhelming dread, or the constant whisper that something terrible is going to happen. He knows that if he can fill a believer's mind with fear, he can distract them from their purpose. The enemy's primary weapon has always been lies. Jesus called him the father of lies. Anxiety often grows louder when those lies are believed, even subconsciously. Lies such as, "You are not safe." "You are alone." "You are losing control." "God is not going to help you." "Something bad is coming." These whispers do not always sound like a voice from the outside. They can attach themselves to the echoes of past wounds, childhood trauma, abandonment, rejection, or unresolved pain.

I experienced this personally during one of the most difficult seasons of my life. At the time, I was carrying enormous pressure. There were battles surrounding our church, financial concerns, opposition, uncertainty about the future, and the weight of leadership. At the same time, old wounds that I thought had been buried began to resurface. The stress became so overwhelming that my mind and body seemed to turn against me. Fear appeared without warning. My heart would race. Waves of dread would come over me for no apparent reason. I knew what God's Word said, and I loved the Lord deeply, yet I found myself in a battle I could not simply think my way out of.

What made the struggle even more confusing was that many of the fears were not based on reality. Nothing catastrophic was happening in that moment, yet my mind continually warned me that disaster was around the corner. Looking back, I can see that anxiety was feeding on a combination of present stress and unhealed wounds from the past. The enemy was taking advantage of both. He was using old pain to reinforce present fear, and present fear to keep old pain alive.

This is why not all anxiety is demonic. Sometimes the mind is responding to grief, loss, stress, unprocessed trauma, or emotional exhaustion. Sometimes anxiety is the body's way of saying it has carried too much for too long. Trauma changes the nervous system. Pain rewires the brain. Abandonment leaves imprints. Childhood wounds leave memories buried so deep that a person does not even realize why they react the way they do. In these moments, anxiety is not always the voice of the enemy. It is the cry of the soul. It is the body trying to protect itself. It is the heart trying to survive.

Yet there are also moments when anxiety is spiritual. Not every fear is psychological. Not every panic comes from trauma. There are times when the enemy attacks us, creating fear that comes quickly, intensely, and without logical cause. There are moments when anxiety rises out of nowhere, when a heaviness enters a room, when a believer wakes in the night with an overwhelming sense of dread, or when a sudden wave of fear hits with no explanation. These moments are not imagined. They are recognized throughout Scripture as spiritual oppression. They are the enemy attempting to gain ground, and bring fear into your life.

One of the greatest challenges believers face is distinguishing between the two. Is this spiritual warfare or emotional trauma? Is this the enemy or is this the result of a wound that has not healed? The answer is often both. The enemy attacks where we are wounded. He targets the places already bruised. He uses our history against us. He whispers into old memories. He strikes the places where we feel least confident, most afraid, or most ashamed. Trauma may open the door. The enemy may step through it. Emotional pain may create cracks. The enemy may exploit them. Neither truth cancels the other. Anxiety can be spiritual. Anxiety can be emotional. Anxiety can be physical. And in many cases, it is all three overlapping at once.

This is why healing must be holistic. Holistic means looking at something as a whole, not just focusing on one part of it. A believer cannot only treat anxiety as demonic or they will miss the places where the heart needs healing. A believer cannot only treat anxiety as emotional or they will miss the spiritual attacks that require authority in Christ. God desires to heal all three parts of a person: the spirit wounded by lies, the soul wounded by trauma, and the body affected by stress and fear. Healing happens when these layers are addressed together, not separately. Prayer is needed, but so is processing. Scripture is needed, but so is support. Deliverance is needed when the enemy attacks, but so is emotional healing when the heart cries out.

The enemy wants believers to think anxiety disqualifies them. He wants them to believe it means they lack faith, or that something is wrong with them. But Scripture shows the opposite. The prophet Elijah, who called down fire from heaven, was so overwhelmed by fear and despair that he begged God to let him die. David, the man after God's own heart, cried through psalms filled with anguish, panic, and trembling. Paul said he experienced fear within and conflicts all around. Jesus Himself sweated drops of blood in Gethsemane, a physical response to overwhelming stress. Anxiety many times is evidence of our humanity.

The enemy also wants believers to feel ashamed of their struggle. Shame keeps people silent. Silence keeps people isolated. Isolation keeps people vulnerable. But Scripture never tells believers to hide their weaknesses. It tells them to bring their weaknesses into the light where God's strength is made perfect. When the enemy convinces someone to hide their pain, he deepens the wound. When he convinces them they are alone, he increases the fear. When he convinces them that anxiety is a sign of failure, he steals their confidence and their joy.

But the truth is that God meets His children in the places they fear the most. He steps into the middle of the storm. He speaks peace into the chaos. He restores the broken parts of the heart and renews the mind that feels overwhelmed. He heals through His presence, His Word, His Spirit, and often through people, counseling, and practical support. He brings deliverance where the enemy has attacked. He brings comfort where trauma has wounded. He brings clarity where confusion has taken root.

The believer's confidence does not come from pretending the battle is not real. It comes from knowing God is greater than every battle. It comes from knowing that no matter how loud the enemy shouts, God's voice speaks louder. It comes from knowing that no matter how deep the wound, God heals deeper still. It comes from knowing that anxiety, whether spiritual or emotional, is not the end of your story. The presence of anxiety does not mean the absence of God. In fact, it is often in those trembling places that God draws closest.

For every believer who finds themselves battling fear, heaviness, panic, or overwhelming thoughts, this truth stands firm: God sees you. God hears you. God understands the layers of your struggle even when you cannot. He knows the difference between spiritual attack and emotional trauma. And He knows how to heal both. He does not shame you. He does not abandon you. He doesn't call you weak. He calls you His. And no attack of the enemy, no wound of the past, and no moment of anxiety can separate you from the love of God or the future He has written for your life.

Healing is possible. Freedom is possible. Restoration is possible. And God will walk with you through every layer of that journey, fighting for you, comforting your soul, and strengthening your mind until peace becomes your reality again.

When Faith Meets the Brain

Many believers are caught off guard the first time they experience anxiety that does not respond instantly to prayer. You love God, you trust His promises, you speak His Word, yet your body can still react with the same physical symptoms even though you know the truth of Scripture. This disconnect between what you believe and what you feel can create confusion. But don't confuse it with a lack of faith, It simply means you are human.

Faith and biology are not at war with each other. They never have been. God created the spiritual world, but He also created the human body. He designed the brain in all its complexity. He formed the nervous system and every pathway that regulates emotion, memory, and fear. God is not threatened by the science behind anxiety. He is the Author of it.

Understanding how faith and the brain interact brings clarity to an experience many Christians do not know how to explain. You can fully trust God and still have a body that reacts to stress. You can walk in obedience and still have neural pathways shaped by past experiences. You can believe Scripture and still have an amygdala that fires too quickly.

When you begin to understand how the brain processes emotion, something remarkable happens. You begin to see it as an invitation for God to meet you in places you never knew needed His touch. Anxiety means there are parts of your internal world that have not yet experienced the safety and healing God intends for you. Faith does not remove the nervous system. Faith teaches the nervous system a new way to live.

One of the most encouraging truths is that prayer itself changes the brain. Neuroscientists call this neuroplasticity, the brain's ability to form new pathways. When you pray consistently, your prefrontal cortex, the part of the brain responsible for regulation, becomes stronger. This makes it easier to calm emotional reactions. At the same time, prayer quiets the amygdala, the brain's alarm system. Studies show that regular prayer reduces the intensity of fear responses, lowers cortisol, and increases the brain's sense of connection and belonging. Prayer is doing far more than moving mountains. It is reshaping the pathways inside your head.

Worship affects the brain as well. When you worship, your brain releases dopamine, the neurotransmitter associated with joy and motivation. Worship lowers stress hormones and activates the parasympathetic nervous system, which signals the body to relax. This is why moments of worship often bring tears, deep emotion, or an unexpected sense of relief. Your spirit is connecting with God, but your nervous system is also responding to that connection. Worship becomes a meeting place between heaven and biology.

Scripture engages the brain in a unique way as well. When you meditate on the Word of God, you are engaging the same neural networks used in cognitive retraining. You interrupt negative thought patterns and replace them with healthier ones. Scripture gives the brain new images, and new truths to hold on to.

David understood this intuitively when he wrote, *"Your word have I hidden in my heart"* (Psalm 119:11). The Word of God was not merely information to him. It was nourishment for his inner world. It was the anchor that kept him grounded when his emotions swayed. Scripture shaped David's brain long before anyone knew what neural pathways were.

Paul says "do not be conformed to the patterns of this world, but be transformed by the renewing of your mind, that you may prove what *is* that good and acceptable and perfect will of God" (Romans 12:2). This verse tells us that the word of God helps us create new patterns of thinking and processing in our mind.

Even breath, something so simple and automatic, plays a

profound role in healing. The breath God gave you is directly connected to your emotional state. Slow, deep breathing activates the vagus nerve, which tells the body it is safe. This is why God often instructed His people to be still. Stillness calms the nervous system. Stillness grounds the soul. Stillness allows the brain to shift from survival to presence. When you breathe deeply during prayer, you are aligning your spirit with God and your body with peace.

There is also power in confession, not the kind that exposes shame, but the kind that releases what has been held inside for too long. When you speak about what hurts, the brain begins to reorganize the emotional memory. What was stored in fear begins to be released. David practiced this in his Psalms. He did not hide his fear or pretend to be strong. He wrote about it, prayed about it and sang about it. Psalm after psalm is evidence of a man healing through honest expression in God's presence. Emotional honesty is one of the deepest expressions of faith because it acknowledges your need for God.

Healing begins when you realize that your biological response is not in competition with your spiritual truth. They are intertwined. God uses both. He speaks peace to your spirit, but He also teaches your body how to rest again. He strengthens your beliefs, but He also rewires your brain. He calms your soul, but He also calms your nervous system.

Faith does not ignore your emotions. Faith brings them

into alignment with God's love. Emotional healing is not always a single moment. Emotional healing is a process where the truth of God gently reshapes every part of who you are.

David once wrote, *"He restores my soul"* (Psalm 23:3). Restoration is not instant. Restoration is careful, patient, and deeply intentional. It involves placing back together what life has scattered. It involves calming what trauma has disrupted. It involves renewing what anxiety has exhausted. And the God who restores the soul also restores the mind, the emotions, and the nervous system.

Faith meets the brain in the place where honesty meets truth, where vulnerability meets grace, and where trauma meets the restoring presence of God. That is where transformation happens. And that is where your healing begins.

Chapter 12

The Spirit Of Fear

There were times in my life when everything looked fine on the outside. Nothing major was going wrong, nothing was falling apart, and yet inside, something felt off. I couldn't explain it. Anxiety show up out of nowhere, and I found myself trying to make sense of it, because it did not seem to match my circumstances. Maybe you have felt that too. Everything looks stable on the outside, but inside there is an unrest thats brewing.

Anxiety has a way of slipping quietly into the mind, settling into the thoughts, and beginning to rehearse worst case scenarios on repeat. It tells us something bad is coming, or that we are not safe. Anxiety does not always come from what is happening around us. Often, it comes from fear that has been allowed to take root within us.

Scripture makes it clear that fear is not merely an emotion to be managed. At times, fear functions as a spiritual influence that presses against the mind and heart. The Bible even identifies fear as a spirit. Paul writes, *"For God has not given us a spirit of fear, but of power and of love and of a sound mind"* (2 Timothy 1:7). This distinction matters. Fear is not only a feeling we experience. It can be a presence we submit to or resist. Power, love, and a sound mind are gifts given by God's Spirit. Fear, when allowed to rule, works in opposition to them.

This helps explain why anxiety can feel overwhelming and intrusive. Fear does not simply suggest thoughts, it tries to take control of them. When fear is treated only as a psychological issue, it is often managed but not confronted. However, when it is recognized as a spiritual force, it can be addressed with spiritual authority. Anxiety loses its grip when the Spirit of God governs what fear has been influencing.

Few biblical stories illustrate this more clearly than the life of Elijah.

Elijah was a prophet who had just experienced one of the greatest spiritual victories recorded in Scripture. On Mount Carmel, he stood alone against hundreds of prophets of Baal and called fire down from heaven to prove that his God was all powerful. Then he killed the prophets of Baal with a sword. Almost immediately afterward. Scripture tells us that when Jezebel heard what Elijah had done, she sent a message threatening his life. *"And when he saw that, he arose and ran for his life"* (1 Kings 19:3). One message was all it took. One voice.

One threat. The same man who had just stood fearless before a nation now found himself running for his life.

Elijah ran until he collapsed beneath a broom tree and prayed for his life to end. *"It is enough! Now, Lord, take my life"* (1 Kings 19:4). Nothing had changed about God's power. Nothing had changed about God's presence. But fear reframed reality in Elijah's mind. Fear told him he was alone. Fear told him he was finished. Fear told him it was over.

This is how fear works. It does not need facts. It only needs our attention. Fear will always say "it is enough". Fear tries to convince us that the end has arrived when God is still writing the story.

What follows is revealing. God does not rebuke Elijah. Instead, God addressed his fear at its root. First, Elijah is allowed to sleep. He is fed. His physical exhaustion is met before his emotional despair is confronted. *"Then as he lay and slept under a broom tree, suddenly an angel touched him, and said to him, 'Arise and eat'"* (1 Kings 19:5). Fear often gains strength when the body and soul are depleted.

After Elijah reaches Mount Horeb, God asks him a simple question. *"What are you doing here, Elijah?"* (1 Kings 19:9). God is not seeking information. He is inviting reflection. Fear had moved Elijah out of position. Fear had relocated him mentally and spiritually. But God was gently calling him back into position.

Then comes the moment many remember. A powerful wind tears through the mountains, but God is not in the wind. An earthquake follows, but God is not in the earthquake. Fire comes next, but God is not in the fire. Finally, Scripture says there is a still small voice (1 Kings 19:12). When Elijah hears the voice of God, his perspective returns. God reminds him that he is not alone. There are still seven thousand who have not bowed to Baal. Fear had told Elijah he was isolated. God revealed he was surrounded. This is what fear tried to do, it tries to isolate you. Yet, truth reconnects us to who God is and to who we are.

I can still remember a time in my life when I felt alone and afraid. I remember telling my wife that I feel alone, that nobody cares about me. Here I was with a large church and hundreds of people who loved me, yet I felt all alone. this is what a spirit of fear will do. Next I started playing scenarios in my mind that the people who loved were going to abandon me.

This is what fear can do. It will ask, "What if?" The spirit of fear tries to get us to focus on outcomes we cannot control. But the Spirit of God centers us on a presence we cannot lose. Jesus addressed fear directly when He said, *"Peace I leave with you, My peace I give to you; not as the world gives do I give to you. Let not your heart be troubled, neither let it be afraid"* (John 14:27). Jesus did not deny that trouble would come.

He promised peace within it. Peace is not merely a feeling to pursue. It is a Person who dwells with us.

Breaking a spirit of fear is not about silencing thoughts through willpower alone. It is about changing which voice we are yielding to. Fear speaks lies. God speaks truth. Fear says we are alone. God promises His presence. Fear says we will not survive this. God assures us His grace is sufficient.

Scripture declares, *"Fear not, for I am with you; be not dismayed, for I am your God. I will strengthen you, yes, I will help you"* (Isaiah 41:10). God Word reminds us that He is always near.

If you are battling fear, it does not mean you lack faith. Elijah did not lack faith. It may mean you are tired, overwhelmed, or listening too long to the wrong voice. God does not abandon His people in moments of fear. He meets them there. The same God who fed Elijah, spoke to Elijah, and restored Elijah is present with you now.

Fear may be loud, but it is not authoritative. Fear may be persistent, but it is not permanent. *"For you did not receive the spirit of bondage again to fear, but you received the Spirit of adoption by whom we cry out, 'Abba, Father'"* (Romans 8:15). Fear may attempt to influence, but it does not get to rule. God is not a visitor in your life. He is your dwelling place.

You are not alone in this battle. The God who walked with Elijah in the wilderness walks with you today. He has not abandoned you, forgotten you, or turned away from your struggle. Even when fear feels overwhelming and the darkness seems endless, His presence remains constant. God never promised that His children would never face fear, but He did promise that they would never face it alone. He is the God who said, "I will never leave you nor forsake you" (Hebrews 13:5). When you cannot see the way forward, He is your guide. When you feel weak, He is your strength. When your heart is troubled, He is your peace.

The fear you are facing today is not greater than the God who holds you. He is with you in the valley, with you in the storm, and with you in the long nights. He stands beside you as your Shepherd, goes before you as your Defender, and surrounds you as your refuge. You may feel alone, but you are not abandoned. You may feel weak, but you are not defeated. You may feel afraid, but you are held securely in the arms of a faithful Father.

So lift your eyes beyond the fear and look to the One who has never failed you. The same God who sustained Elijah will sustain you. The same God who restored Elijah will restore you. This season will not last forever. Fear does not have the final word. Anxiety does not have the final word. Your circumstances do not have the final word. God does. His everlasting presence is with you now. He will be with you tomorrow, and He will remain with you until the day you stand in His presence forever.

Chapter 13

The Moment You Stop Running

There came a point in my life when I realized I could not keep running anymore. I had learned how to stay busy, how to fill my schedule, how to keep moving so I would not have to slow down and deal with what was going on inside of me. For a while, it worked. I could push things aside, ignore the weight, and convince myself I was fine. But eventually, it caught up with me.

The moment I finally slowed down was the moment I realized how tired I really was. Not just physically, but mentally and emotionally. What I had been avoiding did not disappear. It was still there, waiting for me.

Looking back, I can see that anxiety was not just something to fight against. It was an alarm. It was a signal that something deeper needed my attention. It was telling me it was time to stop, slow down, and face what I had been avoiding for far too long.

I reached that point during the season when my anxiety became impossible to ignore. My body was sending signals that my spirit had tried for years to push aside. I had lived most of my life in survival mode. I knew how to work hard, how to endure hardship, how to push through pain, and how to keep going no matter how exhausted I felt. What I did not know was how to be still, how to rest, or how to face the deeper wounds that shaped my inner world. I had built a life on strength, but I had never learned the courage of vulnerability. When anxiety finally forced me to stop running, it felt like I was meeting myself for the first time.

Stopping is hard. When the noise fades, you are left with the echoes of the things you avoided: memories you buried, and wounds you never admitted. This is why many people prefer movement over healing. Movement keeps you numb. But healing requires stillness. Healing requires honesty. Healing requires the willingness to sit with what hurts so God can begin to restore what has been broken.

David experienced this same tension. Throughout the Psalms, we see moments where he could no longer run from what lived inside him. In one of his most honest prayers, he wrote, *"Search me, O God, and know my heart. Try me and know my anxious thoughts"* (Psalm 139:23). This was not the prayer of a man hiding his pain. It was the prayer of a man finally stopping long enough to invite God into the places he once avoided. David allowed himself to be searched. He allowed God to touch the wounds that shaped him. He allowed the hidden places of his heart to become places of healing rather than places of fear.

There is something powerful about stopping long enough to let God search you. It is not about judgment. It is about revelation. It is about letting light into the corners of your heart where pain has been living. When David prayed those words, he was asking God to show him the parts of himself he could not see. He understood that unhealed pain can become a cycle. It influences how you think, how you react, how you relate, and how you see the world. And he knew that breaking the cycle begins with awareness.

When I finally stopped running, I discovered things about myself I had never slowed down long enough to acknowledge. I discovered fears from childhood that still influenced how I responded to stress. I discovered the insecurities that shaped my decisions. I discovered the grief I had never allowed myself to feel. I discovered that many of the pressures I blamed on the present were rooted in the past. And for the first time, I allowed God to meet me in those vulnerable places.

Stopping does not mean quitting. Stopping means surrendering. It means saying, "God, I cannot outrun this any longer. I cannot carry this without You." It means stepping out of your own strength and into the presence of a God who knows every layer of your pain and every detail of your story. It means trusting that the God who guided David through his darkest moments will guide you through yours.

There is a freedom that comes when running ends. It is the freedom of finally breathing again. It is the relief of no longer pretending. It is the peace of letting God touch the places you once feared would destroy you. Healing does not begin when life becomes easier. Healing begins when you stop running from what hurts. Healing begins when you allow God to search your heart the same way David did. Healing begins when you are honest with yourself and honest with God.

The moment you stop running is the moment you begin to heal. It is the moment the cycle breaks. It is the moment your heart begins to rest. And it is the moment God can finally begin the work He has been waiting to do in you for a very long time.

You do not have to have all the answers before coming to God. You do not have to clean yourself up before entering His presence. You do not have to hide your wounds, your questions, your fears, or your failures. God already sees them, and He invites you to bring them to Him. Healing begins when you stop carrying your burdens alone and place them into the hands of the One who cares for you. Jesus extends this invitation in Matthew 11:28-30: "Come to Me, all you who labor and are heavy laden, and I will give you rest. Take My yoke upon you and learn from Me, for I am gentle and lowly in heart, and you will find rest for your souls. For My yoke is easy and My burden is light."

Perhaps the greatest step toward healing is simply praying, "Lord, here I am. Search me. Reveal what I have been hiding. Show me the wounds I have ignored, the pain I have buried, and the fears I have carried. I surrender them to You." When those prayers are prayed with honesty and humility, God begins to work. He shines His light into dark places, brings truth where there have been lies, and pours His healing into areas that have been hurting for years.

The journey of healing starts with a single act of surrender. Stop running. Come to Jesus. Bring Him the weight you were never meant to carry. Bring Him the wounds that still ache, the memories that still sting, and the burdens that have exhausted your soul. Lay them at His feet and allow Him to give you the rest He promised. The God who sees every wound is also the God who heals every wound surrendered to Him. His grace is greater than your pain, His peace is deeper than your hurt, and His love is strong enough to carry you through every step of the healing process. The invitation still stands today: "Come to Me." And when you do, you will discover that the place of surrender is also the place where healing begins.

Chapter 14

Why Healing Feels Like a Battle

Healing is not always simple, predictable, or easy. Many people assume that once they understand how anxiety works, once they pray, once they begin working on their past, healing should happen quickly. But healing rarely works that way. Healing can be a battle, because your body is trying to unlearn patterns it has lived with for years. Your brain is trying to rewrite old pathways and your heart is learning how to trust again. This takes time, intention, and patience.

One of the reasons healing feels so difficult is that for years, many people learn to survive by suppressing painful memories, ignoring deep hurts, or distracting themselves from unresolved trauma. The pain may seem hidden, but it is not gone. It often remains beneath the surface, influencing thoughts, emotions, relationships, and even physical health without a person fully realizing it.

When you begin the healing process, those buried wounds often start to rise to the surface. Memories you tried to suppress suddenly return. Grief that was never processed begins to make itself known. This can be alarming because many people expect healing to bring immediate relief. Instead, healing often begins by exposing what has been hidden.

This is one reason healing can feel worse before it feels better. It is similar to cleaning a deep wound. Before healing can take place, the wound must be uncovered, cleaned, and treated. The process may be uncomfortable and even painful. But, in many cases, it means you are finally facing what you once had to suppress in order to survive.

The temptation during this stage is to run back to old patterns of avoidance. It may feel easier to ignore the pain, stay busy, numb the emotions, or convince yourself that none of it matters. Yet true healing is found by walking through the pain, not around it.

At our church, we offer a class called Elevate Freedom. This class was designed specifically to help people identify areas of brokenness, unresolved pain, unhealthy patterns, and spiritual strongholds that may be preventing them from experiencing the freedom Christ purchased for them. Time and again, we have watched God bring healing, restoration, and breakthrough to people who were willing to take an honest look at their hearts and allow God into places they had hidden for years.

One of the realities we have observed, however, is that not everyone completes the journey. Some people begin the process enthusiastically, but when hidden wounds start coming to the surface, they become uncomfortable. The moment healing requires honesty, vulnerability, and self-examination, some choose to step away. They stop attending the class. They avoid the conversations. They retreat from the process. Not because they do not want freedom, but because exposing long-buried pain can feel frightening. For many people, the pain they know feels safer than the healing they have not yet experienced.

Yet the truth remains that what stays hidden often remains unhealed. The enemy thrives in secrecy, but healing grows in the light. The very areas we are tempted to conceal are often the places where God wants to work most deeply. Freedom is rarely found by avoiding the wound. Freedom is found by allowing God to touch it.

The wounds that are acknowledged can be healed. The hurts that are brought into the light can be restored. The areas of your life that are surrendered to God can be transformed by His grace. When what used to controlled you from the shadows is finally being brought into the light, healing begins. Do not quit in the middle of the process. Trust the process. Do not run when the pain surfaces. Stay the course. Bring every wound, every memory, every fear, and every burden to God. The breakthrough you are seeking may be waiting on the other side of the very pain you are tempted to avoid.

Another reason healing feels like a battle is because the body resists change. The brain prefers familiar patterns, even unhealthy ones. This is why people often return to old habits, old thoughts, or old coping mechanisms even when they want to change. Healing requires teaching your brain that the unfamiliar can be safe and that the familiar is not always healthy.

Your nervous system also needs time to learn what peace feels like. If chaos was your normal growing up, peace can feel threatening. If you learned to survive by being on high alert, calmness can feel uncomfortable. If you were taught to suppress your emotions, honesty can feel terrifying. Healing asks the nervous system to experience new sensations. It invites the heart to feel things it once avoided. It teaches the body to relax in moments it once braced for impact. This shift is beautiful, but it is also uncomfortable.

Healing feels like a battle because it is a battle. But it is a battle worth fighting. It is not a battle you fight alone. God is not watching from a distance, He is present in every moment of the struggle. He is patient with your process, compassionate toward your pain, and faithful to finish the work He started in you. David wrote, *"The Lord is near to the brokenhearted"*

(Psalm 34:18). He did not say the Lord is near only after you are healed. He said God is near in the brokenness. God is near in the confusion. God is near in the trembling. God is near in the battle.

Healing also feels like a battle because your past and your future are wrestling inside you. The past tries to pull you back with familiar patterns. The future calls you forward with hope and possibility. The present becomes the battleground where change takes place. Every moment you choose honesty over hiding, you are winning. Every moment you choose stillness instead of running, you are growing. Every moment you choose truth over fear, you are healing.

Healing is not linear. You will have days of breakthrough and days of setback. You will have moments of deep peace and moments when old memories rise again. God does not rush the process. He walks with you through it. He guides you gently. He speaks truth to your heart and peace to your nervous system. He restores layer by layer until your soul can breathe again.

When difficult days come, keep moving forward. A hard day does not erase the progress God has already made in your life. A painful memory resurfacing does not mean you are back where you started. It simply means God is continuing His work in another area of your heart. The Great Physician is thorough. He does not merely cover wounds; He heals them.

He does not abandon unfinished work; He completes it.

Take comfort in knowing that God is infinitely patient with you. He is not frustrated by your struggles. He is not disappointed by your weakness. He understands every tear, every fear, every setback, and every battle you face. Psalm 103:14 reminds us, "For He knows our frame; He remembers that we are dust." Your heavenly Father knows exactly where you are in the healing journey, and He is not asking you to heal overnight. He is simply asking you to keep walking with Him.

One day you will look back and realize that the pain that once controlled you no longer has the same power. The wounds that once defined you will become part of your testimony. The fears that once ruled your thoughts will be replaced by a deeper confidence in God's faithfulness. What feels overwhelming today will not always feel this way.

Until then, rest in this truth: you do not walk this road alone. The same God who began the healing work in you is faithful to finish it. He is with you on the good days and the hard days. He is with you in the breakthroughs and in the setbacks. He is with you when you feel strong and when you feel exhausted. His hand has never left you, His love will never fail you, and His plans for your restoration remain unchanged. So take the next step, however small it may be, and trust that God is leading you toward wholeness. He has not brought you this far to leave you now.

Chapter 15

When Wisdom and Healing Meet

For a long time, I refused to seek help. I told myself I could handle it, that I just needed to pray more, push through, and stay strong. As a pastor, I had spent years helping others through their struggles, pointing people to God, praying with them, and encouraging them to trust Him. But when it came to my own internal battles, it was much harder to admit that I needed help.

In many of the circles I had been part of, therapy carried a quiet stigma. It was often viewed as something worldly or unnecessary for a believer. There was this unspoken belief that if your faith was strong enough, you should be able to overcome anything through prayer, worship, and trusting God alone. I had heard this for years, and if I am honest, I believed it myself.

So when I began to consider seeing a therapist, it was not

a simple decision. I wrestled with it internally. I questioned what it meant about my trust in God, about my role as a pastor, and even how others might view me. There was a part of me that wondered if needing that kind of help meant I was lacking somewhere spiritually.

At the same time, I was struggling in ways I could no longer ignore. I knew what I believed, but I also knew what I was experiencing. The truth is, many well-intentioned ideas have caused people, including myself, to struggle in silence. We were taught, directly or indirectly, that needing help like this was not God's will.

So, I made the decision to push past those beliefs and ask for help from a professional. For me, choosing to see a therapist was not a step away from God. It was a step toward healing. If I may, let me be the first one to tell you that there is nothing wrong with talking to a therapist. Now with that said, I would strongly encourage you to seek help from a christian therapist if possible.

God uses doctors, teachers, pastors, mentors, and counselors. He uses gifted men and women to bring clarity, comfort, and wisdom. Throughout Scripture, God partnered with people to bring healing to others. Moses had Aaron. David had Samuel. Paul had Barnabas and later Silas. The apostles were strengthened and encouraged by each other. Healing has always involved community. Restoration has always involved guidance. Therapy simply continues what Scripture has shown from the beginning: God often heals through people He equips.

The belief that Christians should not need therapy usually comes from a misunderstanding of what therapy actually does. Therapy does not replace the power of the Holy Spirit. Therapy does not push God out. It creates space for deeper healing so the believer can hear God more clearly. It helps reveal the internal barriers that keep someone from applying Scripture to the deeper places of the heart. Professional help does not compete with the Holy Spirit. It works alongside the work the Holy Spirit is already doing.

A licensed Christian therapists is trained to understand trauma, emotional patterns, learned behaviors, and the way the mind responds to fear. They help people make sense of what is happening inside so they can walk toward healing with clarity rather than confusion. They help believers identify the roots of patterns that prayer alone may not reveal. They help untangle lies that someone has believed about themselves so that the truth of God's Word can take deeper root. Proverbs 15:22 says, "Plans fail for lack of counsel, but with many advisers they succeed." The Bible does not discourage counsel. It encourages it.

The idea that someone does not need therapy because they have God is incomplete and unhealthy. God is the source of healing, but He often uses practical means to deliver that healing. When someone breaks a bone, they pray for healing and go to the doctor. When someone has high blood pressure, they pray and take the medication that helps their body function. When someone faces financial trouble, they pray for guidance and seek wise instruction. Emotional healing is no different. Therapy in many cases is how we cooperate with God's process of healing.

Now, I will say that some may just need to talk to their Pastor or a spiritual leader who is gifted with wisdom from God. For many, this may be the first step toward healing. Or if your church offers a restoration class, I would encourage you to attend. But even pastors and restoration classes have their limitations. I for one may be able to help someone through spiritual guidance. But there are times where I will refer them to a christian therapist because there need for healing is beyond my scope of knowledge.

Many believers have carried emotional pain for years. They learned to suppress memories, hide trauma, ignore triggers, or bury fear beneath spiritual language. But God did not design the soul to heal through suppression. He designed it to heal through truth. Therapy helps bring truth into the places we tend to keep hidden. It reveals what needs attention so God can restore what has been wounded.

God often uses therapists in the same way He uses pastors,

mentors, and medical professionals. He gives them insight, compassion, and skill. He uses their training to bring clarity and healing. A believer does not have to choose between therapy and faith. The two can work together. Faith provides the foundation. Therapy helps remove the obstacles that keep that foundation from flourishing.

Professional help should never be viewed as worldly. It should be seen as another way God brings light into dark places. It should be embraced as part of the journey toward wholeness. It should be honored as a gift God uses to guide His children toward restoration and emotional freedom. Walking into a therapist's office means you are giving God more room to heal you.

Healing takes courage, humility, and wisdom. Professional help is one of the ways those qualities take shape in a believer's life. God is not threatened by therapy. He is not offended by it. He is not replaced by it. He is the One who walks with you into every session. He is the One who sits with you in the room. He is the One who uses every conversation to bring truth, clarity, and healing to the heart He loves.

I remember when the day finally came for me to sit across from a therapist and begin the work I had avoided for years. I did not walk in with excitement. I walked in because I knew something inside me had reached its limit. I knew I could not keep outrunning memories or pretending I was unaffected by the wounds that shaped me.

I chose a Christian therapist, and I would recommend that to anyone who wants healing without losing the foundation of their faith in God. I needed someone who understood my emotional weight and honored my relationship with God. In those sessions, I did more than talk about trauma. I learned how to take my pain to God honestly. Therapy became a safe place where Scripture, sorrow, and healing could finally meet. Talking about my trauma helped me to draw me closer to Him.

Therapy is not simply conversation. It is a process of uncovering the places we avoid. It invites us to look at the stories we hid because they were too painful. It brings buried emotions to the surface so they can finally be addressed. In that room, I learned to speak openly about experiences that shaped my reactions and the way I saw myself.

The first thing my therapist did when I walked into the office was hand me a journal. She encouraged me to to start writing out all my emotions and pain. Journaling became a powerful part of my healing. My therapist encouraged me to write freely, without filters. That simple act began opening doors inside me that I had kept closed for years. Writing unlocked emotions I had never allowed myself to feel.

Little by little, layers began to lift. Sometimes slowly, sometimes suddenly. I started realizing how much of my anxiety and fear came from unprocessed pain. I began speaking aloud memories I had never acknowledged. And as I did, I felt something shift inside of me. Tears came that I had held back for decades. Those tears brought with it a release.

There is a sacred release that happens when truth is spoken in a safe place. It is the moment your heart stops fighting itself. It is the realization that you no longer need to carry the weight alone. As those layers lifted, I felt lighter. I breathed differently. I thought differently.

Therapy taught me that God heals through process as much as through miracles. He heals through honesty, reflection, and vulnerability. He heals through uncovering what we once buried. Psalm 34:18 says, "The Lord is near to the brokenhearted and saves the crushed in spirit." For many people, therapy becomes the place where that Scripture becomes real.

God was present in every session. He was present in every memory, every tear, every moment of breakthrough. Therapy did not erase my past. It changed the way I relate to it. It helped me understand them. Most of all, therapy created space for God to heal the parts of me I had never surrendered because I never knew how.

For the first time, I felt myself becoming whole from the inside out.

If you find yourself carrying wounds you do not know how to unpack, I want you to know that it's okay to seek professional help. God is with you in the process. He works through counselors, through community, and through the wisdom He gives others. If therapy is part of your healing, trust that God is already prepared to meet you there. You are safe to heal. You are safe to seek help. God is okay with it, and He will walk with you every step of the way.

Chapter 16

A Pathway to Healing and Spiritual Clarity

When my therapist first handed me that journal. It seemed simple, almost too simple. Part of me wondered how writing things down could really make a difference. But I took it home and started writing.

At first, the words did not come easy. I sat there longer than I expected, not sure where to begin. Then slowly, I started writing about things I had not talked about in years. Old pain, past experiences, thoughts I had pushed aside. And once it started, I couldn't stop.

What surprised me was not just what I wrote, but what I felt. Things that had been buried began to surface. Things that had felt confusing started to make more sense. It was like I was finally giving myself permission to be honest, not just with God, but with myself.

Looking back, that journal became more than just pages

filled with words. It became a place where healing started. A place where I could process, reflect, and bring everything before God in a real and unfiltered way.

Although journaling may feel modern, I discovered that the practice is deeply rooted in Scripture. In fact, one of the most profound examples of journaling in human history is found in the Book of Psalms. The Psalms are, in essence, David's journal. They are his unfiltered prayers, his private meditations, his fears, his griefs, his triumphs, his confessions, and his declarations of faith. David did not write for an audience. He wrote for God. He wrote to process what he felt. He wrote to make sense of what he endured. He wrote to get what was living inside him out in plan site.

David's honesty is what makes the Psalms so powerful. He wrote with a raw transparency that shows us what it means to bring our whole selves before the Lord. Sometimes he wrote from a place of deep despair. Sometimes he wrote while overwhelmed by fear. Sometimes he wrote in moments of joy and victory. Through every season, David journaled before God, and God used his words to bring healing, revelation, and strength not only to him but to generations after him.

Psalm 142:2, David writes, "I pour out my complaint before Him; I declare my trouble before Him." This is journaling. This is writing with vulnerability. David is pouring out his words. Every emotion is brought into the presence of

God through writing, and because of this, David finds clarity, comfort, and direction.

In Psalm 62:8, Scripture says, "Trust in Him at all times, O people; pour out your heart before Him." Journaling becomes one of the most practical ways to pour out the heart. When pain and emotions remain unspoken, they often remain unhealed. But when we write, it becomes the doorway to truth.

There is a reason so many of David's psalms begin in distress but end in worship. Journaling helped him shift from emotion to revelation. It allowed him to see God more clearly in the middle of his pain. For example, in Psalm 13 David begins with the haunting question, "How long, O Lord?" Yet by the end he writes, "I will sing unto the Lord, because He has dealt bountifully with me" (Psalm 13:6). The journal becomes a journey. The writing becomes the place where the heart turns from sorrow to praise.

When you journal, you enter that same spiritual process. You give language to your struggles, your anxieties, your questions, your memories, and your pain. The act of writing slows the mind down so the truth can surface. Journaling is not just writing. It is processing, releasing, and inviting God into places you may not have visited in years.

Scripture gives us many examples of writing for the sake of remembering, processing, and drawing closer to God. In

Habakkuk 2:2, the Lord says, "Write the vision and make it plain on tablets." God doesn't just value written reflection. He commands it. Writing becomes a tool for clarity, direction, and obedience. Your journal is no different. It becomes a place where God speaks, where ideas take shape, where healing begins, and where truth becomes visible.

In Lamentations, Jeremiah pours out his grief in raw, poetic form. He writes, "My soul is bereft of peace; I have forgotten what happiness is" (Lamentations 3:17). Yet only a few verses later, after writing through his sorrow, he declares, "But this I call to mind, and therefore I have hope: The steadfast love of the Lord never ceases" (Lamentations 3:21–22). Writing shifted his perspective from despair to hope. Journaling helps you call truth to mind. It helps your spirit remember that God is a good God.

The Bible also emphasizes the importance of remembering God's work. Psalm 77:11 says, "I will remember the deeds of the Lord." Psalm 105:5 says, "Remember the wondrous works that He has done." Journaling becomes a spiritual archive of God's faithfulness. When future storms come, your journal becomes evidence of how God sustained you before. When fear rises, your journal reminds you of the peace God provided in past seasons. When doubt creeps in, your journal becomes testimony.

Journaling also helps untangle the lies that anxiety whispers. It is difficult to challenge anxious thoughts when they remain vague and unspoken. But when you write them down, you can evaluate them through the lens of Scripture. You can confront what is untrue and replace it with truth. Second Corinthians 10:5 says to "take every thought captive," and journaling makes that command practical. You cannot take captive what you cannot name. Writing helps you identify what your mind is saying so that you can shine the light of truth on it.

David often did this in the Psalms. He would write his fear, then he write the truth. He would express his confusion, then declare God's promises. Psalm 42:5 shows this clearly: "Why are you cast down, O my soul, and why are you disquieted within me? Hope in God." David journals his distress, then journals his declaration. This is emotional and spiritual alignment. This is the healing power of writing.

Journaling becomes a sacred conversation. It is your heart speaking and God answering. It is your emotions rising and God meeting you there. It is your confusion coming to the surface and God bringing clarity. Journaling gives God something to work with. When your thoughts are written, God can reframe them.

For many believers, journaling becomes the place where the Holy Spirit brings revelation. You begin writing about a problem, and suddenly an insight surfaces. You pour out your emotion, and the weight begins to lift. You express your confusion, and suddenly Scripture comes alive. This is not coincidence. This is God working through reflection. The Spirit moves when you slow down. The Spirit speaks when you open your heart. Journaling creates the space for that encounter.

There will be days when journaling feels like worship, days when it feels like confession, and days when it feels like survival. All of it matters to God. He is present in every word you write, every tear you shed, every truth you uncover, and every memory you finally allow yourself to acknowledge. Your journal becomes the altar where your soul meets God.

If David had not journaled, we would not have the Psalms. Your journal may never be read by the world, but it will shape your world. It will strengthen your walk with God. It will deepen your understanding of yourself. It will open the doors of healing that have been closed for too long.

Journaling is a spiritual necessity. It is a biblical discipline. It is a tool God uses to bring light into the places we keep hidden. And just as He met David in every psalm, He will meet you in every line you write. Modern neuroscience confirms what Scripture has shown for thousands of years: writing is healing.

Do not wait for the perfect moment to begin. Do not worry about saying the right words. Start with whatever you feel.

Start with whatever rises in your heart. Start exactly where you are. Let your journal become your safe place. Let it become your place of prayer. Let it become the altar where your honesty meets God's healing. Your healing may not come all at once, but it will come. And as you write, the same God who met David in the Psalms will meet you in every line, every tear, and every truth you place on the page. Pick up your pen. Open your journal. Your healing begins with your first word.

How to Journal

Here is a simple model you can use: Write it. Feel it. Pray it. Anchor it.

1. Write It

Write whatever comes to mind. Do not censor yourself. Let your heart speak honestly.

2. Feel It

Allow yourself to acknowledge the emotions attached to what you write. Naming feelings helps them release their grip.

3. Pray It

Turn your writing into a conversation with God.
Ask God

"What do You want to show me?"

"What truth am I forgetting?"

"Where are You in this?"

4. Anchor It

End your entry with Scripture or truth. For example:

"God is my refuge and strength."
"The Lord is near to the brokenhearted."
"I will hope in God."

Your journal becomes a mirror revealing what is inside you and a map guiding you toward healing.

Chapter 17

Faith, Medication, and the Battle No One Sees

During one of the darkest seasons of my life, I made a decision I never thought I would have to make, and that was to go see a doctor because I had reached a point where I could no longer push through what I was feeling on my own, even though I had been praying, believing, standing on Scripture, and doing everything I knew to do spiritually, yet the anxiety was still there, persistent and unrelenting.

When I finally sat in that room and explained what I had been experiencing, the doctor listened carefully and prescribed anti-anxiety medication, which immediately created an internal struggle within me. As a believer, and especially as a pastor, I had always associated strength with trusting God completely, and I found myself wrestling with what this meant about my faith, wondering if I had somehow fallen short or if I had missed something along the way, yet at the same time I knew I was dealing with something real that I could not ignore any longer, and it forced me to confront a deeper truth that many believers quietly wrestle with.

There is a side of anxiety that continues even when you genuinely love God and sincerely trust Him, a side that lingers even after prayer, worship, Scripture, fasting, and every spiritual discipline have been faithfully practiced, and for many Christians the greatest confusion does not come from anxiety itself but from the tension of experiencing real emotional and physical symptoms while still holding on to faith, because it creates an internal conflict that whispers that your faith should be enough.

Yet what I began to understand through that process is that the presence of anxiety does not mean I didn't believe God would take care of me, it simply revealed that my mind was overwhelmed.

Even though we are wonderfully made, we are still human, and humans have limits, and coming to the place where you recognize that limit is a step toward real healing.

There are times when anxiety becomes so persistent that additional support is needed. Medication is one of the tools available to help stabilize the mind and calm the nervous system long enough for deeper healing to begin.

As we step into this part of the conversation, I want to be very clear. This should always be a last resort. I am only sharing this because it was my last resort. I reached a point where prayer, fasting, worship, counseling, and every spiritual discipline I knew were not enough to quiet what was happening inside of me. My mind was overwhelmed, my body was exhausted, and I needed help just to think clearly again. Medication helped me refocus long enough for real healing to begin. It created a window of calm where I could finally breathe, rest, and rebuild.

But it is important to understand that medication is intended to be short term and never a replacement for spiritual growth, emotional work, or the deeper healing that only God can complete. It is a temporary support, not a permanent solution, and it should never take the place of faith, wisdom, or the ongoing process of addressing the roots of anxiety through God's guidance and healthy practices.

Medication does not replace faith, nor does it diminish a believer's trust in God. It simply creates enough internal quiet for the person to think clearly, rest properly, and move forward without being controlled by fear. Medication can provide space for the soul to breathe again. Scripture reminds us that every good and perfect gift is from above, as James 1:17 declares. When used correctly and with wisdom, medication can be one of those gifts.

When we step back and look at the whole picture, we begin to realize that we already embrace medical support in so many areas of our lives. When we have a headache, we take aspirin. When our stomach is upset, we reach for antacids. When our body aches, we do not hesitate to take something that eases the pain. No one questions a believer's faith when they take medication for arthritis, blood pressure, or an infection. The brain is an organ just as real as the heart, the lungs, or the kidneys. When it is overwhelmed, injured, unbalanced, or exhausted, supporting it is simply caring for the body God created.

Still, medication must be approached with caution. It is not something to take lightly or impulsively. It should never be used as a shortcut to avoid emotions, escape responsibility, or numb the heart. There must always be wisdom, counsel, and medical guidance. One thing you have to keep in mind, is that the body can adapt to medication over time.

When this happens, the same dose that once brought relief may not feel as effective. You may notice that the medication no longer produces the same calm, the same steadiness, or the same clarity. This decline can create a very real temptation to take more, in hopes of chasing the relief that once came easily. It is a temptation that is subtle and often rooted in desperation. People simply want to feel normal again. They want the noise inside to quiet. They want to think without racing thoughts. They want to sleep without fear. But taking more than prescribed, even once, can create a dangerous path.

Increasing a dosage without medical supervision can shift a person from support into dependence. It can train the body to expect higher levels of medication and can create complications that make healing far more difficult.

There is another layer of caution that surrounds medicine is stopping the medication too quickly. Many people make the mistake of discontinuing it as soon as they feel better. They assume the anxiety has passed and the medication is no longer needed. However, the body often reacts strongly when medication is stopped abruptly. Withdrawal symptoms can mirror or even intensify the very anxiety someone was trying to escape. This can lead to cycles of stopping, restarting, and stopping again, often leaving the person confused, discouraged, and emotionally exhausted.

I know this first hand. When I stopped taking my medication too quickly, I assumed my strength had returned and the worst was behind me, but what followed was one of the darkest valleys I had ever walked through. The anxiety did not simply return; it came back with a force that shook me. My body trembled, my thoughts raced beyond my control, and my emotions felt like they were collapsing in on themselves. There were nights that felt unbearable and mornings when I wondered how I would make it through the day.

During that time, my wife became my anchor in the storm. She would stay up with me when I could not sleep, praying over me with tears streaming down her face. She told me more than once that she could feel my anxiety as if it were pressing against her own spirit. She prayed with me, she prayed for me, and she cried with me. It frightened her deeply. There were moments when she looked at me with a fear I had never seen in her eyes, afraid she was losing me to something neither of us understood.

At my lowest point, intrusive thoughts began to whisper dark lies. I battled thoughts I never imagined I would face, thoughts that terrified me and made me question whether I would ever climb my way out of that place. Yet even there, in the shadows of my own mind, God met me. He guided me back to the support I needed, including medical help, honest conversations, and the slow, steady process of rebuilding what had been shaken.

Looking back, I can see clearly what I experiencing. It was a physical and emotional crash that required compassion, care, and professional wisdom.

This is why medication must be handled carefully and prayerfully. Faith is not reckless. Faith is responsible. Faith does not ignore what the body needs. Faith uses wisdom and follows guidance. Faith understands that God heals in many ways and often through a combination of spiritual, emotional, and physical care. Medication can help calm the body, but only God can heal the soul. Medication can quiet symptoms, but only God can transform the heart. Medication can bring temporary balance, but only God can bring lasting renewal.

For the believer, it is essential to remember that God remains the source of peace. Scripture says, "My peace I give to you," in John 14:27. Medication may support someone during a season, but it cannot replace the peace God gives. It cannot become the foundation of hope. It cannot become the first place someone turns in times of distress. God must remain the center, the anchor, and our refuge. Medication may create space for healing, but God completes the work.

For anyone considering medication, the path forward should be prayerful and careful. Seek God first. Seek counsel. Seek wisdom. Involve your doctor. Move slowly. Stay anchored in Scripture. And remember this truth: needing support is okay. Your faith is not measured by whether you need medication or not, It is measured by whether you continue trusting God through every part of the process.

Chapter 18

The Setbacks That Shape You

One of the most discouraging moments in the healing journey is the setback. You can be doing everything right. You can be praying, journaling, worshiping, and giving God access to the deep places of your heart. Then suddenly it happens. Anxiety rises again. Fear resurfaces. An old memory appears out of nowhere. You feel overwhelmed for reasons you cannot explain. And in that moment, the enemy whispers the lie that you are failing, that you are going backward, or that nothing is changing. But let me encourage you, setbacks mean you are human. They mean your heart is learning, your brain is being renewed, and your body is adjusting to a new way of living.

Healing many times is not a staircase. Sometimes, it is a winding path. Some days move you forward quickly. Some days are slower. Some days may even circle you back around so you can heal the parts you missed the first time. None of these days are wasted. The nervous system does not change in one moment. It changes through repeated experiences of safety, truth, and connection. This is why the moments that feel like setbacks are often the moments your brain is learning to release old patterns.

It may take some time for you brain to start changing and start moving in the right direction. Your brain has spent years, maybe decades, responding a certain way. It has learned to expect danger and to remain alert. When you introduce healing into your life, the brain does not instantly accept it. It evaluates it. It tests it. It checks to see whether peace is safe. This is why old patterns sometimes return. They are the brain's familiar pathways. Healing creates new pathways, but the old ones do not disappear in an instant. They gradually weaken over time as new patterns become stronger.

David experienced setbacks throughout his life. One moment he was confident and full of courage. The next moment he was overwhelmed by fear or sorrow. Psalm after psalm reveals this. In one prayer he wrote, *"The Lord is my shepherd, I shall not want"* (Psalm 23:1). In another moment he cried, *"Why have you forgotten me? Why must I go about mourning"* (Psalm 42:9). David did not spiral because of his feelings. He offered them to The Lord, and through that honesty, God began to reshape him.

Setbacks reshape you too. They expose the places where you still need comfort. They uncover the wounds that still need healing. They reveal the lies that still need truth. They create dependence on God rather than on your own strength. They soften your heart. They deepen your understanding of God's faithfulness. They strip away imperfections and make room for grace.

Setbacks are often the moments when God does His deepest work. You may feel like you are falling apart, but God sees it differently. He is clearing away old debris. He is loosening the grip of emotional memories. He is strengthening the parts of you that will carry you further. He is teaching you to trust Him not only when life feels calm, but when life feels confusing. Healing is not proven in the moments you feel strong. Healing is proven in the moments you feel weak and still choose to keep going.

Setbacks also teach your brain something essential. Every time you come out of a difficult moment, your nervous system learns that the anxiety did not destroy you. You survived it. You moved through it. You prayed through it. You did not run. You did not fall apart. You came out on the other side. Each time this happens, your amygdala becomes less reactive. The fear-based pathways lose strength. The new pathways of safety and presence grow stronger. You are literally training your brain to trust again.

This is the hidden side of healing. The moments that feel like setback are often the moments when growth is happening beneath the surface. When David wrote, *"This poor man cried, and the Lord heard him"* (Psalm 34:6), he was testifying to the setbacks he lived through. He was not describing a life without emotional trouble. He was describing a God who met him in the middle of it. David was not shaped on the mountaintops. He was shaped in the caves, the valleys, the nights of trembling, the mornings of sorrow, and the seasons of unanswered questions.

You are being shaped the same way. Every setback is a teacher. Every tear is a seed. Every moment of weakness is an invitation for God to strengthen what has been fragile inside you. It requires persistence. It requires honesty. It requires the willingness to get up again and again, even when the path feels long.

You are not going backward. You are becoming deeper, wiser, stronger, and more whole than you have ever been. God is using set-backs to shape you into someone who can stand firm. The setbacks that once discouraged you may one day become the stories that encourage others.

And when you look back, you will see that every setback carried you forward.

Chapter 19

Learning to Feel Safe Again

One of the greatest challenges for anyone who has lived with anxiety, trauma, or chronic stress is learning how to feel safe again. You can be surrounded by people who love you, living in a peaceful place, trusting God, and still feel unsafe on inside. This is because safety is not only an external condition. It is an internal experience.

For years, I thought safety came from my environment. If certain problems were solved, if certain pressures disappeared, I believed I would finally feel safe. But safety does not begin around you. Safety begins within you. And when the nervous system has been shaped by fear, instability, trauma, or constant pressure, it takes time to relearn what safety feels like.

Feeling safe is not something you decide. The body learns safety through repeated encounters with peace. It learns safety through consistency. When your nervous system has spent years in survival mode, the absence of danger can feel abnormal.

This is also how Post-Traumatic Stress Disorder (PTSD) often develops. PTSD is not simply a memory problem; it is a survival response that becomes deeply ingrained within the nervous system. After a traumatic event—or repeated traumatic experiences—the brain learns to remain on high alert. It begins scanning constantly for threats, even when no threat exists. The nervous system becomes conditioned to expect danger because danger was present so often in the past.

Over time, the brain starts associating certain sounds, places, situations, emotions, or even relationships with the original trauma. A particular memory can trigger the same fear response that was experienced during the traumatic event. The brain reacts as though the danger is happening again in the present moment, even when the actual threat is long gone.

Just as repeated experiences of fear taught the nervous system to expect danger, repeated experiences of safety help teach the nervous system that danger is no longer present. Every encounter with God's presence becomes part of re-training the mind and body to live differently.

This is why healing often requires patience. You are not only changing your thoughts; you are teaching your entire nervous system a new way to live. You are teaching your mind that it no longer has to remain on constant alert. You are teaching your heart that it no longer has to brace for impact.

You are teaching your mind that the trauma is no longer in control.

For the believer, this process is not merely psychological; it is deeply spiritual. As you spend time in God's presence, meditate on His Word, and experience His faithfulness day after day, your soul begins to learn what your mind may already know—that you are safe in His hands. The Lord becomes your refuge, your fortress, and your place of rest. Over time, your nervous system begins to align with that truth. The peace of God, which surpasses all understanding, begins to guard your heart and mind in Christ Jesus (Philippians 4:7). Healing occurs as the body gradually learns what the spirit has been trying to believe all along: the danger has passed, God is near, and you are safe.

David understood this long before anyone understood the nervous system. He wrote, *"In peace I will lie down and sleep, for You alone, O Lord, make me dwell in safety"* (Psalm 4:8). Notice how David ties safety to presence, not circumstance. The same David who ran from Saul, hid in caves, and faced betrayal found safety not in his surroundings but in God's nearness. Safety to him was not external protection. It was internal assurance. It was the grounding of his soul. It was the calming of his spirit. It was the quiet conviction that God was holding him even when everything around him felt uncertain.

Safety is learned the same way fear is learned: through repetition. The nervous system rewires itself through experience. Every time you slow your breathing, you teach your body that it no longer has to panic. Every time you speak truth instead of catastrophizing, you strengthen the rational part of your brain.

Learning to feel safe again also means learning to stay present. Anxiety pulls you into the future. Trauma pulls you into the past. Safety exists only in the present. When your body learns to stay here, in this moment, you feel grounded. You begin to notice what is true rather than what is imagined. You begin to respond rather than react. You begin to feel the steadiness of God's presence rather than the shakiness of past fear.

Sometimes learning to feel safe again requires help from others. The nervous system heals in the presence of safe people. This is one reason God designed us for community. Healing is not meant to happen in isolation. Safe relationships teach the nervous system what it never learned in childhood or what trauma took away. Even David had his Jonathan, a friend whose presence strengthened him during seasons when he felt unsafe. This is why I'm adamant about encouraging people to be in church. A healthy Church community can help a person grow in the area of safety. Its also important to spend time with God in prayer and journaling.

Learning to feel safe again also involves letting God into the parts of you that never felt safe before. This means allowing Him to sit with you in your anxiety, your fear, your memories, your tension, and your stories. It means letting Him speak peace to the parts of your heart that panic when life slows down. It means trusting that His presence is not only with you in worship and prayer, but within you in the deepest layers of your emotional and physical experience.

Safety grows as you allow God to shape your internal world. He does not simply protect you from external threats. He calms the internal storms. He quiets the noise that rises inside. He whispers through the chaos, not just to your spirit, but to your mind and your body. Healing is not merely spiritual. Healing is physiological. Healing is emotional. God made you a whole person, and He heals you as a whole person.

Healing is not the absence of fear. Healing is the rebuilding of trust. Healing is the restoration of peace within the body. Healing is the nervous system learning that God is not only the God of your soul, but the God of your biology. Safety is not a destination. It is a relationship. And with each step, each prayer, you are learning to feel safe again.

Chapter 20

The Prince Of Peace

As we come to the end of this book, I want to leave you with one final truth that stands above every strategy, every principle, every insight, and every chapter you have read: peace is not found in a method. Peace is found in a person. His name is Jesus.

Throughout this book, we have explored anxiety from many different angles. We have talked about fear, trauma, emotional wounds, the nervous system, spiritual battles, healing, and recovery. All of those subjects are important because anxiety is often complex. Yet none of them are the ultimate answer. The ultimate answer has always been Jesus Christ. The goal of healing is not simply learning how to manage anxiety better. The goal is learning to walk more closely with the Prince of Peace.

The prophet Isaiah gave Jesus this title hundreds of years before His birth. He called Him the Prince of Peace. Not merely a giver of peace, but the Prince of Peace. Peace is part of His nature. Peace flows from His presence. Wherever Jesus rules, peace follows. Wherever Jesus is welcomed, fear begins to lose its authority. Wherever Jesus is trusted, anxious hearts begin to find rest.

This is why peace cannot ultimately be found in circumstances. Circumstances change. The world around us is constantly shifting. If our peace depends upon things remaining stable, our peace will always be fragile. But Jesus never changes. He is the same yesterday, today, and forever. The peace He gives is anchored not in what is happening around us but in who He is.

When the disciples found themselves in the middle of a violent storm, panic filled their hearts. The waves crashed against the boat, the wind howled around them, and experienced fishermen believed they were about to die. Yet Jesus stood and spoke three simple words: "Peace, be still." Immediately the storm obeyed Him. What is remarkable about that story is not simply that Jesus calmed the storm around them. It is that before He calmed the storm around them, He was already calm within it. The disciples were terrified by what they saw. Jesus rested in complete peace because He knew His Father was in control.

That same Jesus is with you today.

The Prince of Peace is not standing at a distance watching your struggle. He is present in it. He sees every anxious thought. He sees every sleepless night. He sees every fear. He sees the burdens you carry and the battles you fight. He knows the wounds that contributed to your anxiety. He understands the pain behind the fear and the exhaustion behind the struggle. Yet none of it causes Him to turn away from you. He moves toward you with compassion, grace, and love.

Perhaps the greatest lie anxiety tells is that you are alone. Anxiety isolates. It convinces people that no one understands. It whispers that things will never change. It magnifies problems while minimizing God's presence. Yet Scripture continually reminds us that we never face life's battles by ourselves. Jesus promised, "I will never leave you nor forsake you." Those are not merely comforting words. They are a covenant promise from a faithful Savior. There has never been a moment in your struggle when Jesus abandoned you. There has never been a moment when His grace was insufficient for your need.

In my own journey, I have learned that peace is not the absence of difficult emotions. Peace is the confidence that Jesus remains present in the middle of them. There were seasons when I desperately wanted God to remove the struggle immediately. Instead, He often met me in the struggle. I wanted instant relief, but He offered His presence. Looking back now, I understand that His presence was what I needed most. The greatest gift God can give an anxious heart is not always a changed circumstance. Often it is a deeper awareness that Jesus is near.

This is why the invitation of Jesus remains so powerful. "Come to Me, all you who labor and are heavy laden, and I will give you rest." Notice that Jesus does not simply offer answers. He offers Himself. He does not say, "Come to a system." He says, "Come to Me." He does not say, "Come to a formula." He says, "Come to Me." The rest your soul longs for is ultimately found in relationship with Him.

As you close this book, my prayer is not simply that your anxiety decreases. My prayer is that your relationship with Jesus deepens. My prayer is that you come to know Him not only as Savior but as the Prince of Peace. My prayer is that when fear comes, you run to Him. When anxiety rises, you turn to Him. When wounds resurface, you bring them to Him. When uncertainty surrounds you, you trust Him. The closer you walk with Jesus, the more you will discover that His peace is not fragile. It is strong enough to sustain you through every season of life.

So if there is one thing I hope you remember from this book, remember Jesus.

When anxiety speaks, remember Jesus.

When fear rises, remember Jesus.

When your heart is troubled, remember Jesus.

When you feel alone, remember Jesus.

When you do not know what tomorrow holds, remember Jesus.

The Prince of Peace is still on the throne. He is still in control. He is still faithful. And He will carry you safely through every storm until the day you stand before Him in perfect and everlasting peace.

Before you close this book, I want to give you an opportunity to respond to the Prince of Peace. Perhaps you have been searching for peace in relationships, success, money, achievement, religion, or your own efforts, only to find that the emptiness remains. The peace your heart longs for is not found in a circumstance; it is found in a Savior. Jesus Christ loves you, died for your sins, and rose again so that you could be forgiven, restored, and reconciled to God. He is standing at the door of your heart and inviting you into a relationship with Him. You do not have to clean yourself up first. You do not have to earn His love. You simply need to come to Him in faith and surrender your life to Him. If you have never given your life to Jesus, or if you have drifted away and want to come home, I invite you to pray this prayer sincerely from your heart:

"Lord Jesus, I come to You today recognizing that I am a sinner in need of a Savior. I believe that You are the Son of God, that You died on the cross for my sins, and that You rose again from the dead. Today I turn from my sin and place my faith in You alone. Forgive me, cleanse me, and make me new. I surrender my life, my fears, my failures, my past, my present, and my future into Your hands. Fill me with Your Holy Spirit and teach me to follow You. Be my Lord, and my Prince of Peace. Thank You for loving me, forgiving me, and receiving me as Your child. From this day forward, I belong to You. In Jesus' name, Amen."

If you prayed that prayer sincerely, the Bible says that you have been forgiven, made new, and welcomed into the family of God. This is not the end of your journey; it is the beginning of a brand-new life. The Prince of Peace now walks with you. He will never leave you, never forsake you, and never stop working in your life. No matter what battles you may face in the future, you will never face them alone. The same Jesus who saved you will sustain you, guide you, strengthen you, and one day welcome you into His presence where fear, anxiety, pain, and sorrow will be no more. So keep your eyes on Him, trust His promises, and rest in the peace that only Jesus can give.

About the author

Tom Flores is an author, speaker, and pastor of Elevate Life Church in Southern California. He is passionate about preaching faith, healing, and overcoming life's struggles through a relationship with God.

For many years, Tom Flores has encouraged people through ministry, teaching, and outreach, sharing messages focused on restoration, spiritual growth, and learning to trust God through difficult seasons of life.

Tom Flores holds a master's degree in Biblical Studies and two bachelor's degrees, bringing both biblical knowledge and practical life experience into his preaching, writing and teaching.

Tom Flores is married to Heather Flores and is the father of three boys: Thomas, Matthew, and Justin.

For more speaking engagements and more books written by Tom Flores Scan the QR or visit www.tomflores.com